ALSO BY VIVIAN GORNICK

The Odd Woman and the City: A Memoir

In Search of Ali Mahmoud:
An American Woman in Egypt

The Romance of American Communism

Essays in Feminism

Women in Science: 100 Journeys into the Territory

Fierce Attachments: A Memoir

Approaching Eye Level

The End of the Novel of Love

The Situation and the Story:
The Art of Personal Narrative

The Solitude of Self:
Thinking About Elizabeth Cady Stanton

The Men in My Life

Emma Goldman:
Revolution as a Way of Life

Unfinished Business

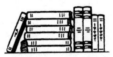

FARRAR, STRAUS AND GIROUX

NEW YORK

Unfinished Business

Notes of a Chronic Re-reader

Vivian Gornick

Farrar, Straus and Giroux
120 Broadway, New York 10271

Library of Congress Cataloging-in-Publication Data
Names: Gornick, Vivian, author.
Title: Unfinished business : notes of a chronic re-reader / Vivian Gornick.
Description: First. | New York : Farrar, Straus and Giroux, 2020. |
Identifiers: LCCN 2019020323 | ISBN 9780374282158 (hardcover)
Subjects: LCSH: Gornick, Vivian—Books and reading. | Women
    journalists—Books and reading. | Books and reading.
Classification: LCC PN4874.G548 A5 2020 | DDC 070.92 [B]—dc23
LC record available at https://lccn.loc.gov/2019020323

Designed by Gretchen Achilles

Our books may be purchased in bulk for promotional, educational, or business use.
Please contact your local bookseller or the Macmillan Corporate and Premium
Sales Department at 1-800-221-7945, extension 5442, or by e-mail at
MacmillanSpecialMarkets@macmillan.com.

www.fsgbooks.com
www.twitter.com/fsgbooks • www.facebook.com/fsgbooks

1   3   5   7   9   10   8   6   4   2

This book is for Randall Jarrell, the man who believed we are devoted to the act of making literature because it leads to the act of reading

AUTHOR'S NOTE

There are sentences, paragraphs—even whole passages in this book—that appeared originally in other publications of mine. I have felt free to "plagiarize" myself, as it were, precisely because my subject here is re-reading, and I have found it useful to "re-read" myself by changing the context within which the thoughts inscribed in these passages first appeared. I sincerely hope the reader will not find this practice off-putting.

Unfinished Business

INTRODUCTION

―――

It has often been my experience that re-reading a book that was important to me at earlier times in my life is something like lying on the analyst's couch. The narrative I have had by heart for years is suddenly being called into alarming question. It seems that I've misremembered quite a lot about this or that character or this or that plot turn— they met here in New York, I was so sure it was Rome; the time was 1870, I thought it was 1900; and the mother did *what* to the protagonist? Yet the world still drops away while I'm reading and I can't help marveling, If I got this wrong, and this and this wrong, how come the book still has me in its grip?

Like most readers, I sometimes think I was born reading. I can't remember the time when I didn't have a book in my hands, my head lost to the world around me. On vacation with family or friends, I am quite capable of settling myself, book in hand, on the living-room couch in a beautiful country house and hardly stirring out into the glorious green for which we have all come. Once, on a train going through the Peruvian Andes, with everyone else ooh-ing and aah-ing out the window, I couldn't lift my eyes from *The Woman in White*. On a Caribbean beach I sat in the blazing sun, Diane Johnson's *Lesser Lives* (an imagined biography of George Meredith's first wife) propped on my knees, and was surprised when I looked up to see that I wasn't surrounded by the fog and cold of 1840s England. The companionateness of those books! Of all books. Nothing can match it. It's the longing for coherence inscribed in the work—that extraordinary attempt at shaping the inchoate through words—it brings peace and excitement, comfort and consolation. But above all, it's the sheer *relief* from the chaos in the head that reading delivers. Sometimes I think it alone provides me with courage for life, and has from earliest childhood.

We lived in an immigrant working-class neighborhood in the Bronx where all needs were met through the patronage of one of the many stores that ran the length of a single shopping street. The butcher, the baker, the grocer, the bank, the drugstore, the shoe repair: all storefront operations. One day, when I was quite small, seven or eight, my mother, holding my hand, walked us into a store I'd never before noticed: it was the local branch of the New York Public Library. The room was long, the floorboards bare, and the walls lined, floor to ceiling, with books. In the middle of the room was planted a desk at which sat Eleanor Roosevelt (in those days, all librarians looked like Eleanor Roosevelt): a tall, bosomy woman with a mass of grey hair piled belle epoque–style on the top of her head, rimless glasses perched high on her incredibly straight nose, and a look of calm interest in her eyes. My mother approached the desk, pointed at my head, and said to Eleanor Roosevelt, "She likes to read." The librarian stood up, said "Come," and walked me back to the front of the store where the children's books were sectioned. "Start here," she said, and I did. Between then and the time I graduated from high school, I read my way around the room. If I'm asked now to remember what I read in that storefront library, I can only recall that I went from Grimm's fairy tales to *Little Women* to *Of Time and the River.* Then I entered college where I discovered that all these years I'd been reading literature. It was at that moment, I think, that I began *re*-reading, because from then on it was to the books that had become my intimates that I would turn and turn again, not only for the transporting pleasure of the story itself but also to understand what I was living through, and what I was to make of it.

I'D GROWN UP in a noisy left-wing household where Karl Marx and the international working class were articles of faith: feeling strongly about social injustice was a given.

So from the start, the politicalness of life colored almost all tangible experience, which of course included reading. I read ever and only to feel the power of Life with a capital L as it manifested itself (thrillingly) through the protagonist's engagement with those external forces beyond his or her control. In this way I felt, acutely but equally, the work of Dickens, Dreiser, and Hardy, as well as Mike Gold, John Dos Passos, and Agnes Smedley. I had to laugh when, a few years ago, I came across an essay by Delmore Schwartz in which he (Schwartz) takes Edmund Wilson to task for Wilson's shocking lack of interest in literary form. For Schwartz, form was integral to the meaning of a literary work; for Wilson, what mattered was not how books were written but what they were talking about, and how they affected the culture at large. His habit, always, was to place a book in its social and political context. This perspective allowed him to pursue a line of thought that let him speak of Proust and Dorothy Parker in the same sentence, or compare Max Eastman favorably with André Gide. For Schwartz, this was pure pain. For me, it was inexpressibly rewarding. And what could have been more natural than that the way I read was the way I would begin to write.

ONE NIGHT toward the end of the 1960s, I attended a speak-out at the Vanguard, a famous jazz club in Greenwich Village. The evening was billed as "Art and Politics," and on the stage was the playwright LeRoi Jones (later Amiri Baraka), the saxophonist Archie Shepp, and the painter Larry Rivers. In the audience, every white middle-class liberal in the city. Very quickly, it became clear that Art didn't stand a chance up against Politics. Jones dominated the event by announcing early that not only was the civil rights movement tired of what he called white intervention, very soon blood was going to run in the seats of the Theatre of Revolution and guess who was sitting in those seats. The place went up in flames, everyone yelling and screaming some version of "Not fair!" all at once—with one voice in particular heard above the rest, crying out, "I've paid my dues, LeRoi. You *know* I've paid my dues!" But Jones, unperturbed and unimpressed by the uproar, continued to explain that we "ofays" had fucked it all up, but when they, the blacks, got there, they would do it differently: smash up the world as we knew it and start all over again. I remember thinking, "He doesn't want to destroy the world as it is, he wants to take his rightful place in it *as it is*, only right now his head is so full of blood he doesn't know it."

I wanted badly to call that out, as everyone else was calling out whatever hurt most, but he terrified me (one can hardly imagine the strength of Baraka's public presence in those painfully inspired days), so I kept silent, went home, and, burning with a sense of urgency I couldn't really account for, sat up half the night describing the entire event from the perspective of my one great insight; and discovering, as I wrote, what was to become my natural style. Using myself as a participating narrator, it was my instinct to set the story up as if writing a fiction ("The other night at the Vanguard . . .") in order to put my readers behind my eyes, have them experience the evening as I had experienced it, feel it viscerally as I had felt it ("I've paid my dues, LeRoi. You *know* I've paid my dues!"), then come away moved and instructed by the poignancy not of Art and Politics but Life and Politics. Although I did not then know it, it was personal journalism that I had begun to practice.

In the morning I put what I had written in an envelope, walked to the corner mailbox, and sent the piece to *The Village Voice*. A few days later my phone rang. I said "Hello," and a man's voice replied, "I'm Dan Wolf, editor of the *Voice*, who the hell are you?" Before I could think I said, "I don't know, you tell me." Wolf laughed and invited me to send him anything else I was working on. A year later I sent him another piece. And I think most of another year passed before I sent in a third.

I had meant it about not knowing who I was. Although at any given moment I could talk a blue streak that often made a listener say "You should write that up," when it came to it, I'd almost invariably suffer a paralyzing case of self-doubt. It was only occasionally that that burning sense of necessity allowed me to bring a piece of work to a satisfactory conclusion. Now, here I was, after the evening at the Vanguard, with an open invitation to face down this painful disability and begin to realize the lifelong ambition of writing professionally. So what did I do? I got married. I got married and left New York to live in a place deep in rural America where every connection I had to writing was dramatically severed. Soon enough, I did get unmarried and I did return to the city, but it was only to wander about, working odd jobs in and around publishing: still an overaged girl refusing to become an adult.

Then one day I walked into the *Voice* office—how I had the nerve to do this I'll never know—and asked Dan Wolf for a job. He said, "You're a neurotic Jewish girl, you produce only one piece a year, how can I give you a job?" I said no, not any more, I'd do whatever he wanted—and, as it turned out, I meant it. Two assignments later the job was mine.

But what, exactly, *was* the job?

The *Voice* was a paper of opinion founded in 1955, at the height of the Cold War, when simply to speak out as a liberal was to be heard as a radical. The key words were "speak out." The paper had a muckraking bent which made its writers, one and all, sound as if they were routinely holding a gun to society's head. In one sense, the enterprise bore a strong resemblance to the social realism of my childhood, so I fit right in. In another, my predilection for personal journalism soon began to complicate the appealing simplicity of "them" versus "us" that ruled *Voice* reporting. Using myself as the instrument of illumination when exploring the subject at hand was forcing on me a growing need to look inward as well as outward: to put the "personal" and the "journalism" together proportionally, figure out how the parts *really* fit together, how the situation *actually* felt on the ground. For the longest time, it seemed, I worked with only partial success to solve this problem. Then the liberationist movements of the 1970s kicked in, politics began to feel existential, and for me the dilemma of how to practice personal journalism was home free.

In late 1970 an editor at the *Voice* said to me, "There are these women's libbers gathering out on Bleecker Street. Why don't you go out and investigate them." "What's a women's libber?" I asked. A week later I was a convert.

Within days I had met Kate Millett, Susan Brownmiller, Shulamith Firestone, and Ti-Grace Atkinson. It seemed as though they were all talking at once, and yet I heard every word each of them spoke. Or, rather, it was that I must have heard them all saying the same thing because I came away from that week branded by a single thought. It was this: the idea that men by nature take their brains seriously and women by nature do not is a belief not an inborn reality: it serves the culture and is central to how all our lives take shape. The inability to see oneself primarily as a working person: *this*, I now saw, was the central dilemma of a woman's existence.

The insight felt new and profound and, above all, compelling. Of a sudden, I saw the unlived lives of women not only as a crime of historic proportion but a drama of the psyche that came brilliantly to life no sooner than the word "sexism" was applied—and that was the word that now governed my days. Everywhere I looked I saw sexism: raw and brutal, ordinary and intimate, ancient and ever-present. I saw it on the street and in the movies, at the bank and in the grocery store. I saw it while reading the headlines, riding the subway, having the door held for me. And, most shockingly, I saw it in literature. Taking up many of the books I'd grown up with, I saw for the first time that most of the female characters in them were stick figures devoid of flesh and blood, there only to thwart or advance the fortunes of the protagonist whom I only just then realized was almost always male. It occurred to me that all my reading life I'd been identifying with characters whose progress through life was at a vital remove from any I would ever make.

The exhilaration I experienced once I had the analysis! I woke up with it, danced through the day with it, fell asleep smiling with it. It was as though revelation alone could deliver me into the promised land not only of political equality but of inner freedom as well. After all, what more did I need than the denial of women's rights to explain me to myself? What a joyous little anarchist I then became! The pleasure I took in the excitement of casting conventional sentiment aside! How blithely I pronounced, "No equality in love? I'll do without! Children and motherhood? Unnecessary! Social castigation? Nonsense!" Life felt good then. I had insight, and I had company. Everywhere I looked I saw women like myself seeing what I saw, thinking as I thought, speaking as I spoke.

Yet, by no means was it all bread and roses. For example, no one had counted on the level of rage the women's movement had released in men and in women alike: strong enough, it sometimes seemed, to set a match to the world. Every day, marriages broke up, friendships ended, family members became estranged—and perfectly decent people were saying and doing the most abominable things to one another. One night at a dinner party, a pair of academics— one a tall, slim woman, the other a short, fat man—were listening intently to a distinguished historian whose field the woman knew well. She was adding her voice to that of the speaker with an occasional question or comment when her colleague impatiently demanded that she stop "interrupting." At any other time within living memory, I was certain, this woman would have fallen silent after receiving such a rebuke. Now, her face hardened and she spat out, "Why, you ugly little man, don't tell *me* to stop speaking!" The table went silent, and within minutes the evening was breaking up. I sat there, stunned. On the one hand, I was thrilled by the woman's outburst; on the other, the loss of civility among us left me with the taste of ashes in my mouth. Who could have imagined that so much hate and fear had been festering for so long inside so many of us.

Within the decade, 1970s feminists came to realize

that while we stood united in political analysis, ideology alone was not about to deliver us from our own damaged selves. Between the ardor of our rhetoric and the dictates of flesh-and-blood reality, it seemed, lay a no-man's-land of untested conviction. We became then, many of us, a walking embodiment of the gap between theory and practice: the discrepancy between what we declared we felt and the miserable complexity of what we actually felt more apparent with each passing day.

The contradictions in my own character rose up daily to plague me, and patterns of behavior I had paid no attention to suddenly loomed large. I had always thought of myself as one of those ordinarily decent people who placed a high value on what is generally called "good character." Now I saw that I did nothing of the sort. In conversation I was cutting and confrontational, at family affairs bored and dismissive, in the office self-regarding to a fault. Although I pined endlessly for intimate connection (I thought) I nonetheless sabotaged one relationship after another by concentrating almost exclusively on what I took to be my needs, not at all on those of my friend or lover. The narrowness of experience to which my own self-divisions had consigned me—how appalling that now felt!

In no time at all an unimagined universe of interiority opened before me, one equipped with its own theory, laws, and language, constituting a worldview that seemed to hold more truth—that is, more inner reality—than any other;

and a drama of internal anguish began to unfold. Every day now I struggled with myself, one part of me pitted against another, reason telling me which behaviors to break free of, compulsion demanding that I ignore reason. Again and again I suffered the humiliation of sustained self-defeat. In the goodness of analytic time it became clear—but this took years to absorb—that insight alone was never going to prove sufficient. The effort required to attain some semblance of an integrated self was going to be the task of a lifetime. As the great Anton Chekhov had so memorably put it, while "others [might have] made me a slave" it was I who must "squeeze the slave out of myself, drop by drop."

Once again, I found myself reading differently. I took out the books—novels in particular—I had read and re-read, and read them again. This time around I saw that whatever the story, whatever the style, whatever the period, the central drama in literary work was nearly always dependent on the perniciousness of the human self-divide: the fear and ignorance it generates, the shame it gives rise to, the debilitating mystery in which it enshrouds us. I also saw that invariably what made the work of a good book affecting—and this was something implicit in the writing, trapped somewhere in the nerves of the prose—was some haunted imagining (as though coming from the primeval unconscious) of human existence with the rift healed, the parts brought together, the hunger for connection put in brilliant working order. Great literature, I thought then and think now, is a record not of the achievement of whole-ness of being but of the ingrained effort made on its behalf.

I STILL READ to feel the power of Life with a capital L. I still see the protagonist in thrall to forces beyond his or her con-trol. And when I write I still hope to put my readers behind my eyes, experience the subject as I have experienced it, feel it viscerally as I have felt it. What follows is a collection of pieces written in appreciation of the literary enterprise as I have encountered it through the reading and re-reading of books that made me feel anew all of the above.

ONE

———

I was twenty years old the day an English teacher put into my hands *Sons and Lovers*. Until then I'd never even heard the term "coming-of-age novel," but I knew one when I saw one; and D. H. Lawrence put the matter so starkly and so dramatically that, even at that tender age, I felt myself communing with the primitive conflict at the heart of the tale. I read the book in one gulp, came back to class entranced, and from that day forward *Sons and Lovers* was biblical text. I read the novel three times within the next fifteen years, and each time identified with another of its major characters: the hero, Paul Morel; his mother, Gertrude; his youthful lovers, Miriam and Clara.

The first time around it was Miriam, the farmer's daughter with whom Paul loses his virginity. I got her immediately. She sleeps with him not because she wants to, but because she fears losing him. During intercourse her terror is such that instead of yielding to the experience, she lies beneath Paul—lost to his own sexual delirium—thinking, Does he know it's me? Does he know it's me? Miriam's primary need is to know that she is desired, and for herself alone. The dilemma was devastating: I felt the heat, the fear, the anxiety engulfing each of these two, but most especially I felt it as though I was Miriam herself. I was twenty years old: I needed what she needed. The next time I read the book I was Clara, the working-class woman who is sexually passionate, wants to engage with erotic life, but still is alive to the potential for humiliation hidden in her need to feel that it is *she* who is being desired and again, for herself alone. The third time I read the book I was in my mid-thirties— twice married, twice divorced, newly "liberated"—and I identified with Paul himself. Now preoccupied with desiring rather than being desired, I gloried in giving myself up to the shocking pleasure of sexual experience itself—rich, full, transporting—imagining myself now, like Paul at the end of the novel, the hero of my own life.

When I came to re-read *Sons and Lovers* again recently, in shall we say my advanced maturity, it wasn't so much that I found I'd gotten many of the details wrong (which I had), but rather that my memory of the overriding theme—sexual passion as *the* central experience of a life—was wrong. This, I now saw, was not really what the book was about; and I found it all the greater and the more moving that I had held it close to my heart all these years for a set of not misinformed but insufficiently informed reasons. It was also one of the first times that I saw clearly that it was I, as a reader, who had had to journey toward the richest meaning of the book.

Set at the turn of the twentieth century in a mining village in the English Midlands, the narrative follows the progress of the Morels and their four children. Gertrude (a schoolteacher of romantic sensibility) and Walter (a fun-loving miner) first meet at a dance, she drawn by his good looks, his gaiety, his talent for dancing while he, in turn, is attracted by her responsiveness to his own sensuality. They develop a passion for each other and they marry. He promises her a house of her own, a good enough income, and tender fidelity. Soon enough, she discovers that on none of these can he deliver: "He had no grit, she said bitterly to herself. What he felt just at the minute, that was all to him. He could not abide by anything. There was nothing at the back of all his show." He, in turn, is startled to find that she cannot bear disappointment well: it turns her bitter and austere. In no time at all, he, bewildered by the constant sense of accusation he now feels at home, escapes to the pub every chance he gets.

Eight years down the road (when the book begins) Mrs. Morel is thirty-one years old, pregnant with her third child, living in undreamed-of poverty both material and emotional, and repelled by her husband whom she (and the children along with her) now experience only as a hard-drinking, violent lout.

As romantic sensibility does not desert Mrs. Morel, it is to her sons—the one daughter has no presence at all—that she inevitably turns for the kind of companionship required to feed emotional starvation. At first William, the eldest, seems to be the one whom she hopes to make a soul mate, but it soon transpires that it is Paul, the second son and our protagonist, with whom she had really been destined to merge. When he is still an infant in her lap, "she felt strangely toward the infant . . . It seemed quite well, but she noticed the peculiar knitting of the baby's brows, and the peculiar heaviness of its eyes, as if it were trying to understand something that was pain . . . Suddenly, looking at him, the heavy feeling at the mother's heart melted into passionate grief." Her soul's anxiety has entered into the babe: at the age of three or four he cries for no reason, grows melancholy for no reason. But the reader understands: the reason is that from birth on, Paul and his mother have been as one.

And now we know this is not exactly "mother love" at work here. These are the thoughts and feelings of a woman who sees her spiritual salvation joined to that of this boy who, in thrall to his mother's adoration, will, as a teenager, declare that he will never leave her but, as he grows to young manhood, ineluctably discover that the life within is pulling him toward the kind of self-discovery that demands she be left behind.

The metaphor Lawrence uses for Paul's wrenching dilemma is, of course, erotic love. As Paul's need for it grows—and the two women, Miriam and Clara, become the instruments of his awakening and initiation—he delves ever deeper into its extraordinary force until he finds that passion has the ability to mimic liberation (this I remembered well), but not actually deliver it (this I did not remember at all). The struggle at the heart of the novel is not between Paul and his mother but between Paul and the illusion of sexual love as liberation. It was this last it was taking me forever to understand.

When I was a girl in the 1950s, the culture was still joined at the hip to those restraints of bourgeois life that kept erotic experience at a distance. This distance fed a dream of transcendence linked to a promise of self-discovery interwoven with the force of sexual passion. Only then we didn't call it passion, we called it love; and the whole world believed in love. My mother, a communist and a romantic, said to me, "You're smart, make something of yourself, but always remember, love is the most important thing in a woman's life." Across the street Grace Levine's mother, a woman who lit candles on Friday night and was afraid of everything that moved, whispered to her daughter, "Don't do like I did. Marry a man you love." Around the corner Elaine Goldberg's mother slipped her arms into a Persian lamb coat and shrugged, "It's just as easy to fall in love with a rich man as a poor man," but her voice was bitter precisely because she too believed in love.

In the ideal life, it was felt—the educated life, the brave

life, the life out in the larger world—that love would not only be pursued, it would be achieved; and once achieved transform existence; create a rich, deep, textured prose out of the inarticulate reports of inner life we daily passed on to one another. The promise of love alone gave us the courage to dream of leaving these caution-ridden precincts in order to turn our faces outward toward genuine experience. In fact, it was *only* if we gave ourselves over to romantic passion—that is, love—without stint and without contractual assurance, that we would have experience.

We knew this because we, too, had been reading *Anna Karenina* and *Madame Bovary* and *The Age of Innocence* all our lives, as well as the ten thousand middlebrow versions of those books, and the dime-store novels coming just behind them. In literature, good and great writers as well as mediocre popularizers had sounded depths of emotion that made readers feel the life within themselves in the presence of words written to celebrate the powers of love. Like everyone else reading *Sons and Lovers* in the mid-twentieth century—and by everyone else I mean the educated common reader—I experienced the book as an essence of this conviction that to know oneself through the senses was to arrive at the heart of human existence.

Now, in late age, marveling at Lawrence's turbulent account of this world-making delusion, I wondered, as I read, how it had escaped me that the characters in *Sons and Lovers* are themselves deeply embittered over the consequences of a life posited on sexual passion—and this almost from the start. While she is still pregnant with Paul, Mrs. Morel begins to wander in her mind. She can barely figure out how she came to be where she is, "and looking ahead, the prospect of her life made her feel as if she were buried alive." Why buried alive? Because, encased as she is in spiritual loneliness, she is drowning in dissociation. "'What have I to do with it?' she said to herself. 'What have I to do with all this? Even the child I am going to have! It doesn't seem as if *I* were taken into account.'"

This was a speech I did not at all recall. And why *would* I have recalled it? It sounded more like a woman speaking in 1970, in the midst of the therapeutic culture, than in 1910 when the Freudian idea of the self was just being born. I had thought of Mrs. Morel as a grim-faced woman whose obsessive involvement with her own betrayed dreams of life has stripped her of dimension; but there she is, conscious, in the midst of the endless quotidian, of that deadliest of deprivations: an inner life gone missing.

Then there is Morel himself. I remembered him as a Caliban, but he is only a childish man whose gift (his only gift) for innocent sensuality has been steadily eroded by the lack of the very thing that could have made him a better person: sympathetic partnership. In his youth, he had been a great dancer with a love of music embedded in a heart that yearned only to be light. But he, too, has been left crying in the wilderness, his head filled with chaos because he is a sentient creature who cannot speak to himself, does not have the words with which to approach his own joyless existence. (Where am I in all this?) It is precisely his inarticulateness that makes it hard for him to come straight home after work, which in turn leaves his wife, even though she now hates the sight of him, doubly trapped in the misery of normalcy outraged: "[She] sat alone. On the hob the saucepan steamed; the dinner-plate lay waiting on the table. All the room was full of the sense of waiting, waiting for the man who was sitting in his pit-dirt, dinnerless, some mile away from home, across the darkness, drinking himself drunk . . . persisting in his dirty and disgusting ways, just to assert his independence. They loathed him."

"They loathed him" cannot be repeated often enough in this book. On page three Mrs. Morel hates Morel; on page five she holds him in contempt; on page eight she loathes him. Then it starts all over again, and these repetitions go on for most of the novel. For a book devoted to "love" the unremitting rage flung down on page after page is sobering.

Yes, they loathed him, but they also *were* him. Paul would rather scrape the skin off his body than admit to any shared characteristic, but—and this I certainly did not remember—he is actually as moody and thin-skinned as his father. "He was the sort of boy that becomes a clown and a lout as soon as he is not understood, or feels himself held cheap; and, again, is adorable at the first touch of warmth." Somewhere within himself Paul must know that all sensuous feeling in him—tender or murderous, ever ready to burst the skin—comes from Morel. But if he had let himself think about the split within himself, it would have made him ill. So Lawrence doesn't make him think about it, but allows the reader to do so.

And then there is William, commonplace William, whose ill-fated life is a small dramatic foreshadowing of erotic disasters yet to come. William has the soul of an accountant: absorbed in his white-collar job in London, which he expects will bring him money and a rise in social status, he quite cheerfully comes home less and less, as children bent on making their way in the city do. But one Christmas, still in his early twenties, he brings home Lily, a secretary to whom he has engaged himself. She is beautiful and he is besotted with her at the same time that he seems permanently irritated by her because she is vain and stupid and—now that he sees her through his mother's eyes—gets horribly on his nerves. Torn apart by the conflict within himself, William quarrels with Lily at the drop of a hat, instantly regrets his bad behavior, then lets his head fill once again with blood: "He repented, kissed and comforted the girl . . . [but] in the evening, after supper, he stood on the hearthrug whilst she sat on the sofa, and he seemed to hate her."

The mother goes into shock at what she sees happening to William—that's how it seems to her, it's happening *to* him, as in a Greek tragedy. "She raked the fire. Her heart was heavy now as it had never been." She herself had been lured into marriage by sexual attraction, but this sort of desperation over its power to enslave—raw, open, uncontrolled—this no one of her generation had ever seen. She immediately recognizes it as world-shattering.

As, very nearly, does William himself. His hunger for Lily is hateful to him: it humiliates him and drives him to act in ways that he himself holds in contempt. He knows that Lily is guilty of nothing more than being herself, yet he cannot refrain from heaping blame on her for his own wretchedness. In a burst of despair he cannot control, he cries out to his horrified mother that should he die, Lily would forget him in a few months, that's how shallow she is.

Passion, passion, passion: hard, mean, wracking: neither sensual nor romantic, only boiling—how could I have forgotten this—passion that is more like war than love: the rawness behind the longing for sexual ecstasy, the depth of its anguish, the fear of ruination, the consequence that can never be undone. It is a stark and unforgiving look we have here at the price sexual hunger could exact a hundred years ago. Inescapably, as I now read on in *Sons and Lovers*, I found myself remembering all those mediocre novels about marriage being written at the same time by H. G. Wells, novels in which the same conflict is often at the heart of the narrative: a working-class boy who longs to rise in the world, but meanwhile is perishing for want of a sexual life and talks himself into marrying the first girl who seems willing to lie down with him if only he will marry her. Invariably, the protagonist in these novels feels dread at committing himself to such a marriage, but the dread loses out to the killing need. It's a situation Wells knows from the inside out; any reader can understand what he is talking about, but his writing is not up to making us feel the anguish inherent in the situation. It is with Lawrence, whose few pages on William and Lily are penetrating, that it is brought to vibrant life. William is a figure much more like a Wells protagonist than he is like his brother, Paul, but it is on his behalf that Lawrence makes us shudder because what he sees in him he sees everywhere and in everyone.

Luckily for the book, William dies not long after the beleaguered Christmas visit, and it will be left to Paul to sort it all out. It is through him that Lawrence will investigate exactly how much devotion either to the flesh or the spirit is required to address what I now saw as the underlying concern of *Sons and Lovers*: how to construct a self from the inside out.

Poor Miriam—and again this I did not remember at all—what a bum rap she gets in this book. She too craves a real life, one that will turn on experiencing herself. Miriam is sixteen when she and Paul meet, brown-eyed, black-curled, beautiful, and inclined toward religion because—as it has been for millions of women before and after—it is the only text available that lifts her from the grubby claustrophobia of an existence whose horizons are right up against her

face. Lawrence sees her situation plainly but—so identified is he with his protagonist—he cannot afford to give her
the sympathy that might make her a more central character
than he needs her to be. So he gives her to us like so:

> *[She was like] such women as treasure religion inside them,*
> *breathe it in their nostrils, and see the whole of life in a mist*
> *thereof . . . She loved tremblingly and passionately when a*
> *tremendous sunset burned out the western sky . . . or sat in*
> *her bedroom aloft, alone, when it snowed. That was life to*
> *her. For the rest, she drudged in the house, . . . quivered*
> *in anguish from the vulgarity of the other choir-girls, and*
> *from the common-sounding voice of the curate . . . [and]*
> *her brothers, whom she considered brutal louts . . . She*
> *hated her position as swine-girl. She wanted to be con-*
> *sidered. She wanted to learn . . . If she could read, the*
> *world would have a different face for her and a deepened*
> *respect . . . Her beauty—that of a shy, wild, quiveringly*
> *sensitive thing—seemed nothing to her. Even her soul . . .*
> *was not enough. She must have something to reinforce her*
> *pride, because she felt different from other people.*

This sense of difference in Miriam is, for Lawrence,
a double-sided coin. Paul shrinks from the religiosity,
but when he sees her in church "his soul stirred within
him," because she seemed "something more wonderful, less
human . . . something he could not get to."

It is interesting—and somewhat painful—to see that this inchoateness in Miriam is treated with suspicion while the same (actually much worse) inchoateness in her brothers—these wild, hardworking farmhands whom Miriam and her mother are constantly trying to civilize through scripture—is analyzed with equanimity. Although these boys "resented so bitterly this eternal appeal to their deeper feelings . . . yet it had its effect on them . . . Ordinary folk seemed shallow to them, trivial and inconsiderable. And so they were . . . painfully uncouth in the simplest social intercourse, suffering, and yet insolent in their superiority" (just like Miriam). "Then beneath was the yearning for the soul-intimacy to which they could not attain because they were too dumb, and every approach to close connection was blocked by their clumsy contempt of other people. They wanted genuine intimacy, but they could not get even normally near to anyone, because they scorned to take the first steps, they scorned the triviality which forms common human intercourse."

These were sentiments Lawrence held—with alternating scorn and compassion—throughout his life, sentiments he feared applied to himself as well as to the people among whom he grew. Thus, for his own purposes, as a writer, he loved, hated, and exploited the Miriams but could neither give nor deny them their due. Instead, he lets Paul Morel drive himself crazy over this dilemma. Hence in one paragraph: "There was . . . the most intense pleasure in talking about his work to Miriam. All his passion, all his wild blood, went into this intercourse with her, when he talked and conceived his work. She brought forth to him his imaginations." But then, Miriam's "intensity, which would leave no emotion on a normal plane, irritated [him] into a frenzy . . . 'Why can't you laugh?' he said. 'You never laugh laughter. You only laugh when something is odd or incongruous, and then it almost seems to hurt you . . . When you laugh I could always cry; it seems as if it shows up your suffering. Oh, you make me knit the brows of my very soul . . . I'm so damned spiritual with you always! . . . and I don't want to be spiritual.'" Then, stricken by his own evil behavior, he sees her with "her soul . . . naked in her great dark eyes, and there was the same yearning appeal upon her."

This habit of Lawrence's, of making the character suffer two and even three reversals of judgment in the space of a single paragraph, is a vivid presence in *Sons and Lovers*. It not only signifies the routine instability of one's actual moods, it nails the torment at the heart of any decision rooted in mixed emotions, and the second—no, not the second, the third—time I read the book it hit me hard. I was now old enough to have experienced many times over the alarming bewilderment of my own erratic behavior—the morning of my first wedding day I was nearly hit by a truck because, as I crossed the street, I was still saying yes, no, yes, no to myself, and failed to stop walking when the light turned red—

and I could feel viscerally the shock of Lawrence's acuity in tracing the staccato nature of emotional confusion.

When at last Paul persuades Miriam to lie down with him it is, of course, a disaster. They fuck for a week—for that is what they do, fuck not make love—but after every episode each is left feeling alone, alone and in despair. We don't know what Miriam is going through, but Paul: "He had always, almost wilfully, to . . . act from the brute strength of his own feelings. And he could not do it often, and there remained afterwards always the sense of failure and of death. If he were really with her he had to put aside himself and his desire. If he would have her, he had to put her aside."

I was nearly thirty the second time I read the book and it was only now that I realized that never for a moment do we see Miriam as she might have seen herself. From start to finish, Miriam remains "other," a creature ever and only instrumental in Paul's battle with his own frustrations. He doesn't know what he wants from her, but whatever it is, he's not getting it and that's all he can concentrate on. "You don't want to love," he raves at her, "your eternal and abnormal craving is to be loved . . . You absorb, absorb, as if you must fill yourself up with love, because you've got a shortage somewhere." Exactly what his mother thinks of Miriam, for her own reasons: "She's not like an ordinary woman, who can leave me my share in him. She wants to absorb him. She wants to draw him out and absorb him till there is nothing left of him . . . she will suck him up." And exactly what I thought the first time I read the book, as I did with all the women in all the books I was then reading—their sole reason for living was to thwart the male protagonist, the one with whom I identified. The possibility that Miriam is laboring under the same blindsided narrowness that hinders Paul and Mrs. Morel—that idea was beyond all of us.

Enter Clara, a working-class feminist of the 1880s who has had enough education and experience so that she, too, feels herself to be "different." Unlike Miriam, Clara is possessed of a haughty reserve that makes her seem mysterious and exciting—even though she's a mass of enervating contradiction: hungry for life yet fearful and suspicious of all who approach her. Nonetheless, she falls for Paul, and she sleeps with him. With Clara he finally knows the rapture of sex; with Clara, he and his partner are drowning together. It is here in bed with Clara that his separation from adolescence—he's twenty-three!—is completed, and the alarming complexity of life, with all its shimmering instability, begins to take hold of him.

When at last Paul and Clara lie down together, the love they make is not only rapturous, the earth moves: "And after such an evening they both were very still, having known the immensity of passion . . . childish and wondering, like Adam and Eve when they lost their innocence and realized the magnificence of the power which drove them out of Paradise and across the great night and the great day of humanity . . . to know the tremendous living flood which carried them always, gave them rest within themselves. If so great a magnificent power could overwhelm them, identify them altogether with itself, so that they knew they were only grains in the tremendous heave that lifted every grass blade its little height, and every tree, and living thing, then why fret about themselves? They could let themselves be carried by life . . . There was a verification which they had had together. Nothing could nullify it. Nothing could take it away."

Oh no?

A mere few months and ten pages later: "Clara knew this held him to her, so she trusted altogether to the passion. It, however," had begun to fail her. "They did not often reach again the height" of the times when they experienced the oceanic. "Gradually, some mechanical effort spoilt their loving, or . . . often he seemed merely to be running on alone; often they realized it had been a failure, not what they had wanted." One night, "he left her, knowing that evening had only made a little split between them. Their loving grew more mechanical, without the marvelous glamor." Within the year they had parted.

It is passages like these two that mark the modernity of the book. Modernity was pushing all writers to put on the page the *entire* truth of whatever it was the writer found festering in the human psyche: not only sorrow and disorder, but sadism, alienation, and the brevity of passion. I now think that Lawrence saw this last by the time *Sons and Lovers* was published—he was then twenty-seven—but the insight alone could not stack up against the pressure of that other thing that he also saw, and that was to be his life's obsession: that to be deprived of experience of the senses, as bourgeois society demanded we be, was truly a sin against life.

Lawrence didn't know any more than Thomas Hardy on this score, or H. G. Wells or George Meredith, for that matter: grown-up writers all. It was simply the urgency with which he insisted on outing what they all knew but could not address directly that set him apart. He was like an abolitionist among antislavery liberals who say yes, slavery is terrible, but in time it will die out, be patient, while the abolitionist says fuck that, now or never, and goes to war.

And it was true: to feel badly but calmly about what is spiritually deforming is the mediocre norm; to rage against it is to become an instrument of revolutionary change. In literature one does that by naming the crime against nature without pity or caution or euphemism; renouncing in no uncertain terms, as W. H. Auden had it, "the laziness or fear which makes people prefer second-hand experience to the shock of looking and listening for themselves."

The third time I read *Sons and Lovers*—it was now the early 1970s—I was in the midst of divorcing my second husband. All around me, friends, relatives, even neighbors felt free to cry at me, "Why are you doing this? What is it you *want*?" The answers, in my own ears, sounded lame. Why *had* I left him? After all, I wasn't married to a man I didn't love, I wasn't being forced to choose between work and marriage, our sex life was fine. But the times were encouraging me to look with new, more unafraid eyes at what I was now feeling driven to do and, somehow, involving myself once again in the harrowing life of the Morels felt intimately related to the task at hand.

I had married—twice!—because when I was young, a woman alone was a woman stigmatized as unnatural, undesirable, un-everything. Yet each time around I discovered that I shrank from being seen as one half of a couple—I actually flinched when addressed as "Mrs."—and while I liked my in-laws well enough, I was intensely bored by family life. Worst of all, there were times when, during a cozy evening at home, alone with my husband, I felt buried alive. The simple heart of the matter was: *I didn't want to be married*. I turned the pages of Lawrence's great novel as though reading Braille, hoping to gain for myself the freedom from emotional blindness the book was urging on its readers.

Within the seven years following the publication of *Sons and Lovers*, Lawrence wrote his two acknowledged masterpieces, *The Rainbow* and *Women in Love*. He said when he started them that he would not again write the way he did of the Morels: graphically and with transparency. No, now he would make what he felt dense with meaning; wild and large and mythic. And so he did. In these books he certainly has got down brilliantly the crime of suppressed feeling—this is where his genius succeeds without parallel. But the part in him that wants to believe in the everlasting good of erotic freedom, there anyone can now feel him plunged in chaos, the writing in these novels in a fever because he suspects that what he insists is true may not, in fact, be true.

Lawrence was writing at the beginning of the Freudian century, the time when Western culture was on the verge of validating his own inner torment. His metaphor—the repression of the erotic—was, in fact, to become the wedge that modernism used to pry open the uncharted territory of human consciousness. If Lawrence were alive today, this metaphor would not be available to him because today all have had long experience of the sexual freedom once denied, and have discovered firsthand that the making of a self from the inside out is not to be achieved through the senses alone. Not only does sexual ecstasy not deliver us to ourselves, one must have a self already in place to know what to do with it, should it come.

That insight, however, was fifty years down the road for all of us. Meanwhile, the longing to forge a life from the experience of a Great Passion—whatever the outcome, whatever the cost—haunted the imagination of those of my generation who pined to live life on a grand scale; and no one pined more for it than high-minded literary young women like myself for whom the ideal carried special weight.

Two

___

In my mid-twenties—still a novice insofar as erotic experience went—I, along with many of my schoolmates, became besotted with Colette, and for many years we read her with the absorption of awestruck students in the presence of a master teacher. That is, we read her to learn better who we were, and how, given the constraint of our condition, we were to live. The condition, of course, was that we were women and, all other things being equal, Love (as we had been told since infancy) was the territory upon which our particular battle with Life was to be pitched. Not another living writer, it seemed to us, understood our situation as well as Colette. No one came even close. In her work we could see ourselves not as we were, but as we were likely to become. It was the potential for self-recognition that made Colette's novels so compelling, sounded depths of understanding that were like nothing we had ever encountered.

She seemed to know everything that *actually* went on inside a woman "in the grip." Her wisdom riveted your eyes to the page, gathered up your scattered, racing inattention, made of *A Woman in Love* as serious a concern for the modern novel as *War and Peace* or *The Search for God*. As you read on in Colette in the 1950s, the noise within died down; at the center, a great stillness began to gather; a point of entry into the human condition was about to be broached.

It was, of course, a given among us that *Chéri* and *The Last of Chéri*—the sequential story of an aging courtesan and her empty-hearted young lover—was Colette's twin masterpiece, but the two books that became imprinted on me were *The Vagabond* and *The Shackle*. Here, Colette dramatized the "condition" in the voice (nakedly autobiographical) of a thirty-three-year-old woman—divorced, sexually experienced, on her own (this identity alone made her thrilling)—for the moment a stage performer on the road with a theatrical troupe, but within herself profoundly at loose ends. Why? Because the question of whether she is to be an independent working woman or a woman given over to Love torments her. In this voice we found a glamorous loneliness, the kind we fantasized as emblematic of the contemporary woman who could throw off the despair of an unhappy marriage, but would then find that along with freedom from the conventions came the potential for another kind of despair, the despair that in Colette's hands became intensely romantic.

For years I had by heart the following passage from *The Vagabond*:

> *Behold me then, just as I am! This evening I shall not be able to escape the meeting in the long mirror, the soliloquy which I have a hundred times avoided, accepted, fled from, taken up again and broken off. I feel in advance, alas, the uselessness of trying to change the subject. This evening I shall not feel sleepy, and the spell of a book . . . even that spell will not be able to distract me from myself.*
>
> *Behold me then, just as I am! Alone, alone, and for the rest of my life, no doubt.*
>
> *Alone! Really one might think I was pitying myself for it!*
>
> *If you live alone, says a friend, it's because you really want to, isn't it?*
>
> *Certainly, I "really" want to, and in fact I want to, quite simply. Only, well . . . there are days when solitude, for someone of my age, is a heady wine which intoxicates you with freedom, others when it is a poison which makes you beat your head against the wall.*

How I resonated at twenty-three to the drama—the sheer poetry!—of this scenario. Renée Néré, the astonishingly forthright narrator of *The Vagabond* and *The Shackle*, is a woman whose fractured identity is central to her existence. She has written books, divorced a despotic husband, gone on the stage, but her hold on her newfound independence is transparently shaky. Take, for instance, the curious business of her relation to her own writing. Although she has published two books, writing is a fugitive activity for Renée. Why? The impulse, quite simply, is not strong enough:

> *From time to time I feel a need, sharp as thirst in summer, to note and to describe . . . The attack does not last long; it is but the itching of an old scar. It takes up too much time to write. And the trouble is, I am no Balzac! The fragile story I am constructing crumbles away when the tradesman rings, or the shoemaker sends in his bill, when the solicitor, or one's counsel, telephones, or when the theatrical agent summons me to his office.*

Again, a situation my friends and I knew all too well . . . and one I was to go on "knowing" for years to come.

Much as she wishes to be "free," and much as she associates freedom with work, Renée's resolve is repeatedly undermined by her conflicted desire for love. Struggle as she may, Colette is saying, a woman is always torn between the longing for independence and the even greater longing for passion. This is the dilemma that commands Renée's real attention. Love has come, and love has gone: she knows its pleasures and its pains inside out. Should it come again, she muses repeatedly, will she give in to the siren song or will she resist it? She thinks about the emotional slavery that accompanies desire: the longings, the anxieties, the potential for humiliation. Still, the lure is powerful. The war within provides the excitement of transgression.

This internal argument about whether or not to resist love is the remarkably sustained subject of the two novels that Renée Néré narrates. In *The Vagabond* she will renounce it, in *The Shackle* she will knuckle under to it. The first gratified us, the second shocked us, but, either way, we were in thrall. What carried the day was the significance, in Colette's hands, of erotic obsession—which of course we were all calling love. In these books Love with a capital L is the glory and the despair equally of a woman's life; to experience both at once (what were we *thinking*!) was to achieve transcendence. "What torments you've thrust me into all over again," Renée cries to the friend who introduces her to a new lover. "Torments," she adds reverently, "that I wouldn't exchange for all the greatest joys." Love is the divine stigma upon which Colette's unique powers of observation were ever trained.

When I came to read these books again for the first time in a half century, I found the experience unsettling. The wholly unexpected occurred: I came away with the bad taste of revised feelings in my mouth. This time around I found myself thinking, How brilliantly Colette evokes Renée—the pathologic insecurity, the endless fantasizing, the morbid preoccupation with aging—but how shallow her situation seems now. Repeatedly, Renée's reflections lead back only and ever to a self that remains unknowing—and clearly are the thoughts of a writer who knows no more than her characters know.

Most striking, for me—the single greatest change, in fact, in my feeling about these novels—was the sense I now had that everything was taking place in a vacuum. When I had read Colette before, the entire world seemed to collect around what I took to be the narrator's wisdom. Now that wisdom seemed narrow and confined. Vanity alone gives her whatever insight into an affair she may gain. While she cannot see that she makes instrumental use of her lovers, she can easily see that she herself has no reality for them and, in her thoughts, she is quick to condemn them for an emotional shallowness she cannot spot in herself:

"How is it that he, who is in love with me," she thinks of Max, her lover in *The Vagabond*,

> *is not in the least disturbed that he knows me so little? He clearly never gives that a thought . . . [never] does he show any eagerness to find out what I am like, to question me or read my character, and I notice that he pays more attention to the play of light on my hair than to what I am saying . . . How strange all that is! There he sits close to me . . . [but] he is not there, he is a thousand leagues away! I keep wanting to get up and say to him: "Why are you here? Go away!" And I do nothing of the kind. Does he think? Does he read? Does he work? I believe he belongs to that large rather commonplace class of persons who are interested in everything*

and do absolutely nothing. Not a trace of wit, a certain quickness of comprehension, a very adequate vocabulary enhanced by a beautiful rich voice, that readiness to laugh with a childish gaiety that one sees in many men—such is my admirer.

In *The Shackle*, Renée is four years older, now retired from the stage, even more unhappily experienced, and even more openly at loose ends. What is there to do but fall into an affair with Jean, a man she could describe much as she did Max, except that now the association is nakedly sexual, and thus unavoidably instructive: "Our honest bodies have clung together with a mutual thrill of delight they will remember the next time they touch, while our souls will withdraw again behind the barrier of the same dishonest but expedient silence . . . We had learnt already that embracing gives us the illusion of being united and silence makes us believe we are at peace." But when the fog of sexual attraction lifts, and they lie there, face-to-face, the same strangers they were before they took off their clothes, for the first time she becomes thoughtful: "I have insulted this lover . . . by giving him my body and supposing that this was enough. He has returned the insult . . . for nothing is exchanged in the sexual act . . . our love which had begun in silence and the sexual act was ending in the sexual act and silence."

In this passage Colette lays out the anxiety of infatuation inflicted on all who suspect that (marvelously, terrifyingly) they are only a catalyst for another's desire. This anxiety is the thing Colette knows through and through—the shrewdness at the heart of all her fame—and clearly the source of her narrator's obsessive preoccupation with aging.

In the earliest pages of *The Vagabond* Renée stares pitilessly into the mirror. She is thirty-three years old, and the dreaded decline is already eating at her. At the end of the novel when Max finally proposes marriage, promising lifelong security, she breaks off the affair with a letter of explanation very nearly unequaled in world fiction:

I am no longer a young woman . . . Imagine me [in a few years' time], still beautiful but desperate, frantic in my armor of corset and frock, under my make-up and powder . . . beautiful as a full-blown rose which one must not touch. A glance of yours, resting on a young woman, will be enough to lengthen the sad crease that smiling has engraved on my cheek, but a happy night in your arms will cost my fading beauty dearer still . . . What this letter lacks is . . . all the thoughts I am hiding from you, the thoughts that have been poisoning me for so long . . . Ah! How young you are. Your hell is limited to not possessing what you desire, a thing which some people have to put up with all their lives. But to possess what one loves and every minute to feel one's sole treasure disintegrating, melting, and slipping away like gold dust between one's fingers! And not to have the dreadful courage to open one's hand and let the whole

*treasure go, but to clench one's fingers ever tighter, and to
cry and beg to keep . . . what? a precious little trace of gold
in the hollow of one's palm.*

Who but Colette could have etched this portrait—acid on
zinc—of a woman staring into the hell reserved for women
alone. And who but Colette could have failed so entirely to
unpack it. Why, I found myself saying to her, have you not
made larger sense of things? Yes, I have from you the incomparable feel of an intelligent woman in the grip of romantic
obsession, and that is strong stuff. But today sexual passion
alone is only a situation, not a metaphor; as a story that begins and ends with itself, it no longer signifies. Let me put
it this way: What young woman today could read Colette as
I read her when I was young? The question answers itself.

Once and once only did Colette come close to using erotic
love as a means to an end rather than an end in itself, and
then, oddly enough, it was through the remarkable figure of
the androgynous Chéri, who, upon my re-reading of the *Chéri*
books, came to seem emblematic of that which I now suspected formed the subtext that lay, untransformed, beneath
the surface of what Colette had ever been writing about.

The story is simplicity itself. The place is Paris, the
time the turn of the twentieth century. Léa, rich and beautiful, a retired courtesan of forty-nine, is living with Chéri,
a boy-man of twenty-five. Léa's wealth derives entirely from
the men whose mistress she has been over the many years

of her phenomenally successful career. The only world she knows is that of other women like herself, confined to the society of one another because no other society is open to them. Chéri is the beautiful, petulant, emotionally arrested son of one of these aging courtesans: as vain, sensual, and materialistic as his mother. Léa has known him all his life. When he was nineteen and she forty-three, sexual attraction had flared between them, and Léa had taken Chéri to live with her. All these years they have suited each other down to the ground. For each, the world beyond immediate desire does not exist.

As the story opens, however, Chéri—who has now lived with Léa for six years—is about to agree to an arranged marriage between himself and the daughter of one of his mother's very rich friends (another retired courtesan), which means that he and Léa are facing the breakup of their arrangement. He pleads with her to understand: much as he adores being with her, he cannot remain her sex toy all his life. Of course, she replies, of course. Go, you must go.

Chéri does marry, whereupon both he and Léa fall into a bout of suffering neither could have imagined themselves capable of; in the event, each had fallen in love for the first and only time in their vacuous lives. After a year of separation, Chéri appears in Léa's bedroom at midnight, declaring himself unable to live without her. They fall into each other's arms, make passionate love . . . and then comes the dawn. While Léa is happily planning to take up their old life together, Chéri suddenly sees that he is in bed with an old woman. Then she sees what he sees. Twenty extraordinary pages follow—the pacing is literary perfection—that trace the time over the space of a morning wherein both characters realize they must part for good.

Five years pass during which the Great War has taken place, and the world that sheltered their cynical innocence has turned to ash. Now, unexpectedly, Léa retreats into the background, and it is Chéri who takes center stage. He has returned from the trenches emptied out: a walking dead man. Nothing and no one can rouse a grain of feeling in him or gain a moment of sustained attention. His old appetite for cars, clothes, and women now holds no appeal for him. He lives with his wife, but instead of looking at her he looks through her. He no longer drinks wine, water alone will do. Every day he dresses, eats breakfast, and leaves the house as though with a destination, only to drift through the streets of the city. Eventually, he becomes an opium addict and, in short order, a suicide.

Behind the vacancy in Chéri's eyes lies a depth of emotional disconnect that, as Colette depicts it, suddenly seems shockingly old; not just old, ancient. It's as though the war has made manifest what had been there from birth on, not only in Chéri but in humanity itself. Thirty years down the road, after another world war, Chéri will morph into Camus's stranger. For now, in 1922, he is marking existential time.

When *The Vagabond* was published in 1910, André Gide

sent Colette a letter of extravagant admiration, declaring it a perfect book. For the next forty years her work would be received in the same spirit by every leading literary light throughout Europe and America. She was beloved not only for her mastery of the French language but also because her books persuaded her readers that she was naming something fundamental and immutable in the human makeup that had not before been named—and to a certain extent she was. But now, well into the twenty-first century, readers like me came to feel that she had not properly identified the malaise central to her work. Upon re-reading the *Chéri* books I now realized that the anomie in Chéri himself is at the heart of Colette's concerns. Anomie is behind the intensity of Love with a capital L. Anomie is why her characters have all buried themselves in eroticism. It is out of anomie that the relation to sensual feeling becomes so all-enveloping it leads Colette to label the shudder of orgasm "the little death."

Anomie and desire: a specialty in French literature that can be traced back at least as far as the 1792 publication of *Les Liasons Dangereuses* and carried forward at least as far as the mid-twentieth-century work of Marguerite Duras. For, after all, what is the work of Marguerite Duras if not an ongoing study of desire linked intimately to self-estrangement? With one important complication: as Duras is writing well into the Freudian century, it was impossible for her to not trace the origins of emotional disconnect to the family romance gone viciously wrong.

THREE

———

Very early in my life it was too late. It was already too late when I was eighteen. Between eighteen and twenty-five my face took off in a new direction. I grew old at eighteen . . . But instead of being dismayed I watched this process with . . . interest . . . The people who knew me at seventeen, when I went to France, were surprised when they saw me again two years later, at nineteen. And I've kept it ever since, the new face I had then. It has been my face . . . It's kept the same contours, but its substance has been laid waste. I have a face laid waste.

The narrator in Duras's novel *The Lover* could easily have encountered Chéri in the Paris flat where he regularly took opium and at last committed suicide: they are two of a kind. I, however, could never have understood this before I myself became old enough to re-read first Colette and then, in turn, Duras, in the light of insight only years of living could have supplied.

When I was eight years old, my mother cut a piece out of a dress I had been longing to wear to a friend's birthday party. She grabbed a pair of sewing scissors and sliced the part of the dress that would have covered my heart if, as she said, I had had one. "You're killing me," she always howled, eyes squeezed shut, fists clenched, when I disobeyed her or demanded an explanation she couldn't supply or nagged for something she wasn't going to give me. "Any minute now I'll be dead on the floor," she screamed that day, "you're so heartless." Needless to say, I did not go to the party. Instead I cried for a week and grieved over the incident for fifty years.

"How could you do that to a child?" I asked in later years, once when I was eighteen, again when I was thirty, yet again when I was forty-eight.

The odd thing was that each time I raised the incident my mother would say, "That never happened." I'd look at her then, more scornfully each time, and let her know in no uncertain terms that I was going to go on reminding her of this crime against childhood until one of us was dead.

As the years passed and I regularly brought up the memory of the dress cutting, she just as regularly denied its veracity. So we went on, with me not believing her, and not believing her, and not believing her. Then one day, quite suddenly, I did. On a cold spring afternoon in my late fifties, on my way to see her, I stepped off the Twenty-Third

Street crosstown bus in New York, and as my foot hit the pavement I realized that whatever it was that *had* happened that day more than half a century ago it wasn't at all as I remembered it.

Migod, I thought, palm clapped to forehead, it's as though I was born to manufacture my own grievance. But why? And hold on to it for dear life. Again, why? When my hand came away from my forehead, I said to myself, So old and still with so little information.

"I'VE WRITTEN A GOOD DEAL about the members of my family," Duras tells us early in *The Lover*, "but then they were still alive, my mother and my brothers. And I skirted around them, skirted around all these things without really tackling them . . . What I'm doing now is both different and the same. Before, I spoke of clear periods, those on which the light fell. Now I'm talking about the hidden stretches of that same youth, of certain facts, feelings, events that I buried."

For years this was Duras's mesmerizing subject, inscribed repeatedly in those small, tight abstractions she called novels, and written in an associative prose that knifed steadily down through the outer layers of being to the part of oneself forever intent on animal retreat into the primal, where the desire to be at once overtaken by and freed of formative memory is all-enveloping; in fact, etherizing.

The time in *The Lover* is the early 1930s, the place In-dochina. A fifteen-year-old French girl stands alone on the deck of a ferry crossing the Mekong River from Sadec, a working-class suburb, into downtown Saigon. She is dressed provocatively in a tattered silk dress held together with a boy's leather belt, gold lamé high-heeled shoes, and a man's fedora, brownish pink with a broad black band running round the base of the brim. On the deck behind her stands a limousine with a twenty-seven-year-old Chinese man, thin and elegant, sitting in the back, watching the girl. He gets out of the car, comes over to her, begins a conversa-tion, trembles as he lights a cigarette, and offers to drive her wherever she is going. She agrees at once and climbs into the car. The man will fall into an amazing passion for the girl, for her thin, white, child-woman's body. The girl's absorption in her own responsiveness will become as rapt as his passion—more so. An affair begins that ends when she is sent to France at seventeen, in possession of the face she will bear for the rest of her life.

What the girl learns during this affair is not only that she is a catalyst for desire but that she herself is aroused by her own powers of arousal. It's a talent: one around which to organize a life. She listens hard when her Chinese lover tells her she will never be faithful to any man. She can feel the rightness of what he says, knows already that it's only the power of desire, not any particular person, that will ever hold her: desire that overwhelms and then ravishes; desire that blossoms through a woman's body, is realized through a man's penetration, and burns them both into oblivion.

Beneath the heat that the girl both generates and shares in, a cold, marvelous detachment is crystallizing. Desire, she can see, is the hunger through which she will come to understand the instrumental nature of human relations. That understanding, she also sees, will become her ticket out. The year and a half with the Chinese lover is the crucible in which this knowledge is fired.

Duras worked this material for thirty years in one fictional abstraction after another. A life in service to desire only confirmed what she had learned in the shuttered room in the Chinese quarter in Saigon in 1932: that she was alone, alone was what she was, and never more so than in pursuit of the pleasure unto death. The irony—disconnect drives one to pleasure; pleasure acts on one like a drug; to be drugged is to feel the disconnect even more acutely— struck her as existentially profound. Consequently, her skill at entering into the complicated addictiveness of erotic love, and drawing the reader inside with her, proved immense. The narrating voice in *The Lover* actually replicates the narcotic lull of desire itself—a thing even Colette could not manage—at the same time that somewhere inside that voice can also be heard the sorrowing sound of one who is using desire to avoid rather than to illuminate. But now, thirty years after the book's publication, it was to this sound—the sound of avoidance—that I found myself resonating.

Repeatedly, in the pages of *The Lover*, the reader is beckoned toward and then deflected from that primitive brutishness Duras called her family: the mother a widowed schoolteacher drowning in depression, the younger brother a sweet slow-witted boy, the older a murderous bully. Regularly, this unfortunate group of misfits, locked together only by ties of blood, retreats into the bitter inexpressiveness of those who experience themselves as permanently marginal:

> *Never a hello, a good evening, a happy New Year. Never a thank you. Never any talk. Never any need to talk. Everything always silent, distant. It's a family of stone, petrified so deeply it's impenetrable. Every day we try to kill one another, to kill. Not only do we not talk to one another, we don't even look at one another. Looking is always demeaning. We're united in a fundamental shame at having to live. It's here we are at the heart of our common fate, the fact that all three of us are our mother's children.*

The emotionally absent mother with whom the narrator is more than half in love, the gangster-ish older brother she fears and loathes, the softly helpless younger one by whom she is erotically moved—to this constellation the reader's attention is repeatedly drawn, and from it just as repeatedly torn away. We feel the narrator's acute loneliness in its midst, but this is a condition she cannot address directly. Instead she indicates, through an interlude here and there, the mad joy that overwhelms her when, on occasion, the mother emerges from her soul-destroying depression, and the girl is penetrated through by a vision of the what-might-have-been:

> *I can't really remember the days. The light of the sun blurred and annihilated all color. But the nights, I remember them. The blue was more distant than the sky, beyond all depths, covering the bounds of the world. The sky, for me, was the stretch of pure brilliance crossing the blue, that cold coalescence beyond all color. Sometimes, it was in Vinh Long, when my mother was [only] sad she'd order the gig and we'd drive out into the country to see the night as it was in the dry season. I had that good fortune—those nights, that mother. The light fell from the sky in cataracts of pure transparency, in torrents of silence and immobility. The air was blue, you could hold it in your hand. Blue. The sky was the continual throbbing of the brilliance of the light. The night lit up everything, all the country on either bank of the river as far as the eye could reach. Every night was different, each one had a name as long as it lasted. Their sound was that of the dogs, the country dogs baying at mystery. They answered one another from village to village, until the time and space of the night were utterly consumed.* I had that good fortune—those nights, that mother.

THE PASSAGE GOES ON so long because Duras cannot bear to part from the memory of a time and place in which all that was supposed to knit up a growing creature's sense of world and self was, for one memorable moment, richly present. Paradoxically, it is also the moment when she is keenly reminded that she has, in fact, been born into loss and abandonment, a prison sentence from which there is no hope of parole.

I have read this passage again and again as the years have gone on, each time returning in spirit to the day my mother—I know, I know, it never happened—cut my heart out of the dress I was meant to wear to the party, each time imagining I would enter more fully into the psychic chaos woven into this memory, thereby coming out the other side a free woman. But no sooner do I come close than I, like Duras, veer away. Unlike her, I do not double back into the infatuation with desire that I now see as calculated not so much to obscure as to confirm the emotional free fall to which she had become devoted; even as I conclude that I, too, must be trapped in that selfsame devotion since my grown-up understanding doesn't seem to yield release from the narcissistic wound any more than Duras's lifelong plunge into erotic oblivion freed her.

FOUR

——

Between what we know and what we cannot hope to know about how we come to be as we are lies an emotional dumping ground into which exceptional writers pour all the art they are capable of making. Duras was one of these writers. Another was Elizabeth Bowen, whose power I felt when I was young, but whose value I did not grasp until I was old. Quite early I gulped down three of her major books—*The Death of the Heart*, *The House in Paris*, *The Heat of the Day*—and then never looked at another word she wrote. I thrilled to the sense of mystery inscribed in Bowen's inordinately original sentences, and to the feeling that something profound was being alluded to in them, but what exactly it was, if my life had depended on it, I could not have described. I remember following the sentences, often with a finger on the page, like a child or a non-English speaker, as though struggling to pick out meaning from an unknowable language.

But oh, those sentences!

Of the social incapacity of one character Bowen writes: "Vague presence, barely a silhouette, the west light sifting into her fluffy hair and lace wrappings so that she half melted, she gave so little answer to one's inquiry that one did not know how to approach." Of another's: "He had a way of looking down while he spoke as though his thoughts were under his eyelids." Then again: "From her marriage a kind of vulgarity Julian's tentativeness aroused in her had been absent, and that year when, however little she knew of Henry, she had best known herself, had a shadowy continuity among her impressions." And here's one describing what it felt like for a character coming into London's Euston Station late during a war-dimmed night: "Recognition of anybody by anybody else seemed hopeless—those hoping to be met, hoping to be claimed, thrust hats back and turned up faces drowningly."

What I could not see in those far-off years was that Bowen was slowing the narrative down with her involuted syntax so that the reader would come under her spell while she labored to get on paper an emotional experience for which there were perhaps no words—or never the right words, or words she couldn't put in the right order—but one that nonetheless haunted her writing. Then, one day, not too long ago, I came across something the American poet Adrienne Rich had written about Emily Dickinson that struck me forcibly, and suddenly, there, front and center in my mind, was Elizabeth Bowen. What Rich had written about Dickinson was this: "I learned from her that there are extreme psychological states that can be hunted down with language. But that language had to be forged— found; made—it was not in the first words that came to mind." I went to my bookshelves, picked up a Bowen novel, and started reading.

On the instant, the text seemed to decode itself: its mission if not its meaning coming clear. Within months I was able to see that for thirty years and more she had created stories and novels meant to acquaint the reader with the power of the one thing—the extreme psychological state—that she deeply understood: namely, that fear of feeling makes us inflict on one another the little murders of the soul that anesthetize the spirit and shrivel the heart; stifle desire and humiliate sentiment; make war electrifying and peace dreary. One other thing I saw: she was one of those novelists whose work, taken as a whole, was a naked demonstration of the psychological damage that often provides the nerve current running steadily beneath the surface of a writer's prose.

Bowen's 1948 novel, *The Heat of the Day*, was composed during the Second World War but completed only after the war when, as she said, she understood better—not completely, only better—what she had been writing about. Set in London in the fall of 1942, it is preoccupied with the unknown within ourselves breaking through during a time of devastation, revealing the fatal lack of fellow feeling beneath the civilized surface we assume as a second skin.

In this novel, Stella, a forty-year-old divorcée, is in love with Robert, a survivor of Dunkirk whom she has met during the Blitz. In the midst of the affair, Harrison, a mysterious intelligence agent, materializes to tell her that her lover is a traitor. Stella refuses to believe him, but as the bombs fall nightly on London, Harrison's menacing presence, now almost a daily reality, begins to eat into the oldest of her anxieties. When he insinuates that the war is only the evil of our own inner lives made manifest, she is pierced by the memory of her own past treacheries—that is, her own failures of feeling—and realizes that "she could no more blame the world than one can blame any fellow-sufferer: in these last twenty of its and her own years she had to watch in it what she felt in herself—a clear-sightedly helpless progress toward disaster. The fateful course of her fatalistic century seemed more and more her own: together had she and it arrived at the testing extremities of their noonday. Neither had lived before."

In a certain sense, all in the novel is tending toward the hour when the protagonist understands her own contribution to world despair—and that hour, metaphorically speaking, is noon because that is the time of day when the sense of aliveness is keenest in London in 1942; after that, one is only waiting for the bombs to fall. Yet Stella's insight has not the power to determine her on a redemptive course of action any more than the horror of the Blitz had the power to maintain its initially high level of psychological terror. Remembering the first bombings in the autumn of 1940, she recalls the uniqueness of that time almost nostalgically: "Never had any season been more felt . . . No planetary round was to bring again that particular conjunction of life and death; that particular psychic London was to be gone forever; more bombs would fall, but not on the same city. War moved from the horizon to the map. And it was now, when you no longer saw, heard, smelled war, that a deadening acclimatization to it began to set in."

This, in Bowen, is a signature passage. The acclimatization to deadened feeling—in war or in peace—is her great subject. For her, this is the enemy of life, the criminal charge she brings against the human condition: that which allows us to adapt ourselves to the atrophied heart. Herein lies the inborn tragedy of this, our one and only life.

SHE WAS BORN IN 1899 in Ireland into Anglo-Irish aristocracy, and grew up in a cold, drafty manor house set down in a rainy, fogbound land, among people locked into a rigid sense of the responsibilities of privilege and tradition. Many of these people were brooding, strong-willed, emotionally intemperate; yet they feared impropriety more than death itself. As is said of a character in Bowen's second novel, *The Last September*, "Life was to him an affair of discomfort, but that discomfort should be made articulate seemed to him shocking." From the start, she had all the metaphors she needed.

When Elizabeth was five years old, her father had a mental breakdown from which he never fully recovered. When she was thirteen, her mother died of cancer. After that she lived among relatives and in boarding schools, feeling obscurely humiliated—even, as her biographer, Victoria Glendinning, puts it, "disfigured"—by her orphaned state. It was then that she came to experience the relief as well as the isolation of guarded feelings. Years later, Bowen identified this period of her life as "the beginning of a career of withstood emotion." From here on in, she—like most of her characters—would become an intimate of "life with the lid on."

The novel that is almost encyclopedic in presenting a full range of characters to flesh out the consequences of life with the lid on is *The Death of the Heart*, published in 1938. Mr. and Mrs. Quayne and their son, Thomas, are leading a proper suburban existence when suddenly, in his late fifties, Mr. Quayne kicks over the traces and has an affair with Irene, a young woman working in a London flower shop. When Irene becomes pregnant, Mrs. Quayne cheerfully expels him from the family home not because her heart is broken but because Mr. Quayne's situation is morally (that is, socially) unacceptable to her. Quayne, Irene, and Portia, their love child, then, as in a nineteenth-century novel, exile themselves to the Continent and spend the next fifteen years wandering about Europe. Both parents die and the sixteen-year-old Portia is sent to live for a year in the Regent's Park home of Thomas, her businessman half brother. However, neither Thomas nor his wife, Anna, is familiar with any degree of normal emotional expressiveness—in fact, the mere idea of such expressiveness makes each of them ill—and the home they have made for themselves is steeped in a silent propriety that serves them as social beings while masking a multitude of hungers and disappointments neither would know what to do with if brought out into the open. Soon enough Portia becomes desperate to figure out why in this house there are "no limits to the loneliness she could feel, even when she was feeling quite resigned."

The catalyst, however, for her ultimate mortification is Eddie, an old college friend of Anna's brother. Eddie had once been a brilliant, beautiful scholarship boy longing to make his way among the rich and the wellborn at Oxford, many of whom had initially found him amusing—"he had a proletarian, animal, quick grace"—and then abruptly dropped him. His sense of insult is profound but instead of walking away from the source of the offense, he clings to whatever remnant of social connection remains available to him. Glued to the edge of a world that will never welcome him as an equal, he gradually becomes less and less real to himself while everyone else, of course, becomes even more unreal. Soon enough, Eddie is as emotionally detached as Adam probably was ten minutes after he'd eaten the apple.

Detachment makes Eddie unreliable, but it is the emptiness within that makes him dangerous. When he meets Portia at the house in Regent's Park, he courts her by persuading her that they are twins, similarly adrift in the brutish world of the unresponsive bourgeoisie. She, pathetically grateful for his attention, assumes a bond of love has formed between them. For a while Eddie pursues the relationship because her naivete allows him to "look right through her . . . without being made shamefully conscious of the vacuum there must be in his eyes." In time, of course, betrayal is a foregone conclusion.

Yet the appeal of Eddie is central to the strength of the book. Although ostensibly an adult, he is actually a true Bowen child, of whom there are many. As with Portia in *The Death of the Heart*, Lois in *The Last September*, Davina in *The Disinherited*, Leopold in *The House in Paris*, in Eddie's presence we are face-to-face with the human fallout at the center of each of Bowen's novels. In him, we feel a frightening innocence—the innocence of stunted empathy— lying just beneath the damage that has been done to each of the children, and that each in turn is destined to inflict on those who love them.

———

MY OWN EDDIE was a man I met at the age of eighteen (when I could easily have doubled for Bowen's Portia), and to whom I remained in thrall for decades.

Daniel, ten years older than I, was darkly handsome, extraordinarily bright, and possessed of a soft, soulful kind of courtesy that never failed to make me feel loved. But the real strength of the attraction between us was rooted in shared sensibility. In this regard Daniel and I were brilliantly matched. Ours was a communion of mind and spirit that Wordsworth might have admired. The conversation between us was its own work of art. We walked together by the hour, discoursing ardently on life, love, literature, each of us yearning, as in a Russian play, toward the remarkable intensity produced by the words that passed between us. This intensity brought peace, joy, excitement—in bed, on the street, at the breakfast table—a depth of well-being I didn't know was missing from my life until suddenly it was there: in Daniel's presence.

Yet, it was also true that from our earliest time together, he sent such mixed signals about who and what he was that often, in the years following our breakup, I would wonder who that benighted girl (me) had been who had indulged in such willed blindness. When we met he told me three things about himself: one, he had been married and was now divorced; two, his parents were living in Europe;

three, he was an ex-alcoholic. I soon discovered that he had been married twice not once, his parents were living in Kansas City not abroad, and on occasion he'd astonish me by belting down a drink. Also, he often didn't call or come when he said he would, or he'd arrive two, sometimes three hours late with some disheveled account of his whereabouts, his eyes shining with delight at now—at long last!—being in my company. Within minutes he had led us away from his delinquency into some newly absorbing conversation in which I clearly was an invaluable participant. How he glowed when he spoke—and I responded poetically to what he said. "My beautiful, marvelous girl," he would invariably beam, "you are life itself!" As I was besotted, I routinely chose to ignore that about Daniel which was transparently alarming. But perhaps *chose* is the wrong word.

IN 1923 BOWEN married Alan Cameron, an education administrator for whom she felt friendship not passion, and with whom she maintained a civilized connection until his death thirty years later. In the interim she had affairs, many affairs. "Sensation," she once said, "I have never fought shy of, or done anything to restrain." In 1941, however, in London, in the middle of the Blitz, she met Charles Ritchie, a thirty-five-year-old Second Secretary at the Canadian High Commission, and with him she fell deeply and irrevocably in love. For Bowen the affair was life-changing; for the unmarried, womanizing Ritchie it was only one among many that he habitually—even troublingly—conducted. Ten months after he and Bowen had met, Ritchie was writing in his diary, "Elizabeth is sad because she loves me more than I love her. It is sad for me too in another way."

Charles Ritchie was Bowen's Eddie come to life. He was not only smoothly intelligent and well-educated, he was charm itself, could talk to anyone anywhere and make them feel they were persons of interest and value; in fact, almost nothing and no one could hold either his attention or his affection for very long. Although Ritchie would never have dreamed of breaking openly with the conventions of his class, in their presence he was made dangerously restless. In 1939, at the age of thirty-three, he was already confiding to his diary, "Family life makes me long for the brothel or the anchorite's cell." There resided within him a vast emptiness which he, too, medicated with sensation. He was attractive to women, and sleeping with them was his drug of choice. From the start, he was routinely unfaithful to Bowen.

Nevertheless, their arrangement prevailed until death did them part. Ostensibly, the affair lasted because Bowen persisted in seeing Ritchie in an heroic light and he, in turn, fell in love with her view of him. But the real dynamic at the heart of their lifelong attachment was that each had recognized something crucial about themselves in the

other—the disfiguring power of "withstood emotion"—
and longed for rescue from its arid fate.

This longing, unevenly shared as it was, sealed a bond
between Bowen and Ritchie that was made dramatic by
the extraordinary combination of need, cynicism, and
self-deception upon which the whole affair fed. In a book
called *Love's Civil War*, published in 2008 by Victoria Glendinning, we have a selection of Bowen's letters to Ritchie,
and those diary entries of his written around the same time
that she was writing these letters. Together, they reveal a
fifteen-year period of her writing passionate letters (actually the same passionate letter) over and over again, while
he, at the same time, is confiding to his diary his bottom-
less dismay over his own spiritual dissoluteness. I choose a
few selections randomly from the years 1945 to 1955, to
demonstrate the astonishing disparity at any given moment
between what he was thinking and feeling while she was
fantasizing and effusing.

- *Ritchie*: "I don't think of E as much as I did. I don't
  even think about myself . . . How long can I stand the
  neatness and emptiness of my life?"
- *Bowen*: "Dearest . . . I think of you so much and love
  you so much . . . this past year has been rather like a
  year on the screen . . . one week differentiated from
  another [only] by your letters."
- *Ritchie*: "Nothing gloomier than this Christmas has

ever happened to me . . . I suppose someday this Death of the Heart, this paralysis of the mind, this dreary vacuum will end . . . The trouble is that when I begin to ask myself the question: What woman do I love? I am overcome by a sort of mental dizziness . . . I feel capable of loving any woman—up to a point—and in one way or another."

· *Bowen*: "My darling . . . Our love is like something that we have given birth to: it has an independent existence of its own, outside temporary anguish and loneliness. It is like an angel . . . able to comfort us and bless us."

· *Ritchie*: "Coming round the corner . . . to go up to my office, I thought that what I would like would be to find myself in a big double bed with a woman, with the curtains drawn and pink-shaded lights, and to fuck and smoke a cigarette and talk a little and . . . drink some champagne . . . and then do it all over again."

· *Bowen*: "I am torn and demented by my longing for you . . . Oh my darling, what a year for us to have had! We are always near to each other, close to each other, all the week round, every week, but naturally this sense of each other floods in most at weekends, doesn't it."

· *Ritchie*: "With me love for a woman is always linked with a need to betray that love: a compulsion which I dread and desire."

- *Bowen*: "[There are times when] I begin to feel almost ill with longing for you, and life becomes an almost unbearable strain."

It wasn't long before I realized that Daniel was a pathological liar. If he went out for a newspaper, he said he was going for cigarettes. If he said he was working late, he was probably at a movie, if having dinner with one friend more often than not it was with another. It was as though it was important that no one knew where or what he was doing at any given moment. The lying went hand in hand with an equally pathological unreliability. Waiting for him in a public place—store, restaurant, library—was almost certainly a prescription for disaster.

I was so unaccustomed to such behavior that at first I was only startled, and the first few times merely demurred. Then I remonstrated, then I grew exasperated, then I fell into a rage. "Don't you see how *insulting* this is," I would cry, "how discounted you make me feel?" Sometimes I wept or screamed or withdrew. Nothing I did reached him. Invariably, he would stare at me or hang his head or murmur feeble words of apology, but always he looked puzzled. He genuinely could not fathom why I was taking on so.

One evening at a party given by some acquaintances of mine, I came out of the bathroom in a somewhat darkened part of the apartment where the party was taking place, to find Daniel and the hostess in a clinch. I must have cried out because they broke apart and the woman fled. I still remember my heart pounding in my chest and my head feeling like it was about to explode.

"Are you sleeping with her?" I asked.

"No," he said.

"Are you thinking of sleeping with her?"

"Not especially. I was just curious. What are you getting so excited about?"

"What am I getting so excited about!"

The thing I remember most from that incident was how devoid of all affect Daniel's entire demeanor—face, voice, body—remained throughout this exchange. For the first time, it occurred to me that emotionally he was somewhere on some other planet.

That night, Daniel confided, quite casually, that he envied me the strength of my feelings. When I asked him what he meant by that, he said that from the time he could remember he himself seemed to have nothing that resembled an ordinary complement of emotions. "Whatever it is that people feel when they're happy, sad, confused," he said, "I don't. I don't feel it. I never have. It's as though there's a leak somewhere in me, and it all got drained out."

"But," I said, "when I tell a joke you laugh. When that girl in the wheelchair came into the restaurant you rushed to help her find a seat. When we make love you're passionate."

His smile was rueful: "That's just me passing for normal. I've studied people for years to see how they act in various situations . . . and I've taught myself to imitate them. I've slept with women who've told me I'm a good lover (*you've told me I'm a good lover*) but, as we all know, the body responds even when the brain doesn't. No sooner do I achieve orgasm than I'm wishing myself gone because then I must demonstrate the tenderness I never feel, yes, even with you. In the end they all leave me, as you will leave me, and y'know, when you do I won't even feel lonely. I'll just feel weary. Weary to death. You know that word, inanition? It's got my name on it."

Suddenly, my young heart was flooded with luxuriant pity. I saw him then as a stricken creature stigmatized by some heroic woundedness; a sacrifice, even, to existential damage; poetic in his affliction; even bearing somehow— and here's where the appeal grew dangerous—some mythic burden of redemption for the rest of us. I vowed silently never to desert him.

Over the years, Daniel betrayed and deceived and defrauded me countless times with open infidelities, public embarrassments, ruined vacations; even embezzled bank accounts. Yet, repeatedly, I was seduced anew, the combined power of his life-giving conversation coupled with the pitiable vacancy at his center holding me fast.

What I failed to register throughout those years was that I had become addicted to a peculiar sense of well-being that came only when Daniel and I were in harmony and deserted me when we were estranged. It was as though knowing him had brought into consciousness some primitive set of hungers that I could neither identify nor hope to satisfy on my own. At those times I felt a kind of drift within myself I had never before experienced. If I had but realized it, I was in thrall to some romantic ideal of trust between us (the one he routinely betrayed) that provided all the excuse I needed to persist in the delusion that I was grounding myself, all the while I remained in free fall.

BOWEN HAD ACTUALLY been writing Charles Ritchie into her characters long before she met him; and nowhere more so than in Max, a protagonist in *The House in Paris*, published in 1935 and one of her more tragic explorations of life with the lid on.

The house belongs to Mme Fisher and her daughter, Naomi. To make ends meet, the two women take in upperclass English or American girls spending a season in Paris. Fifteen years before the book opens (sometime in the 1920s), the English Karen Michaelis, aged eighteen, is one of these girls. She and Naomi become fast friends, and talk endlessly about Max, a darkly unapproachable young man of French-English-Jewish extraction who works in a bank and comes to the house to visit Mme Fisher.

Five years later Max and Naomi show up in London, now engaged to be married. Karen, too, is engaged to be married: to Ray, an Englishman of her own class. Neither

Max nor Karen feels passion for the people they are to marry, and on this visit they realize that they are, and always have been, painfully attracted to each other. A few weeks later they meet in secret, spend a night of love together, agonize over their star-crossed situation, and part. Returning to Paris, Max breaks his engagement to Naomi, is taunted by Mme Fisher, a horrifying self-hatred overcomes him, and he commits suicide. Karen, meanwhile, is left pregnant, has a nervous breakdown, gives the baby up for adoption, and marries Ray.

In Bowen's talented hands this melodramatic tale becomes a metaphor for all in life that can hardly be expressed, much less realized. As it is Max not Karen whom life has already twisted out of shape, it is he who bears the burden of articulating the hopelessness within which they are caught. He begins by describing how he came to be engaged to Naomi.

A born outsider (not for nothing that drop of Jewishness), he has been adrift within himself all his life: a man in his own eyes a bad lot, on the one hand cautious, on the other sly; despairing of life on the margin, tormented by inappropriate desires, never for a moment able to make peace with himself. One day, Max tells Karen, he and Naomi were both in the sitting room of the house in Paris, speaking together as they always had. She was sewing, he lying wearily about. She encouraged him to unburden himself to her, and as he spoke she let her pity for him shine through. Suddenly, Max says, "I looked back at my humiliations, my ridiculousness and self-deceptions, and dreaded others. You do not know what it is to be suspected and to know why. What it is to have no wall to put your back against." He saw then that Naomi's pity "was the only pity I did not resent . . . I went across to her chair and asked her to marry me."

As he speaks, Karen sees that at the same time that Max understands the unholiness of his alliance, both to Mme Fisher and to Naomi, he also grasps the strength with which he is compelled to cleave to it; the dread he feels at being left alone with himself: the self that isn't there.

You do not know what it is to be suspected and to know why.

Of all the characters in Bowen's work to whom I have resonated, it is Max above all who makes me feel I stand at the edge of the abyss. Max through whom the primitive fear of consciousness itself comes most alive; the fear rooted in the suspicion that should we get to the heart of things we will find: nothing.

ONE NIGHT a few years ago Daniel suddenly turned up on my doorstep, wanting to know why I had let him hang around for so long. "Ever figure out what was in it for you?" he asked.

FIVE

———

After Bowen, it came to me that the word "dread" seems to apply most often when the story in question turns on a tale of self-estrangement; when it turns on a tale of cultural estrangement the word that leaps to mind is "angst." Angst, of course, eats away at the soul every bit as much as does dread, but it lends itself to different literary concerns. With angst, the tropes of modernism take a back seat, as those in its grip, so far from being preoccupied with existential nothingness are intent on making eloquent the despair of exclusion.

Mine was the last generation of children born in America to the Jewish Europeans who arrived in this country around the turn of the twentieth century. To a large extent, we remained shaped, throughout our lives, by our parents' anxiety-ridden experience of life on the periphery and, collectively speaking, began quite early to set down a literary record of what it meant to be Jewish-in-America: how it felt to be pushed to the margin, generation after generation. The story was first told through straightforwardly immigrant novels like *The Rise of David Levinsky* (1917), then continued with the self-consciously poetic *Call It Sleep* (1934), and concluded in the 1950s and '60s with the work of Saul Bellow and Philip Roth who brought to the enterprise a language-changing brilliance that made literary history. After that, assimilation did its work and the experience as a whole failed to capture the interest of serious writers, none of whom could bring the necessary outrage to bear on what was no longer a live reality; outrage, of course, being the sine qua non of Jewish-American writing.

Lately, I've found myself thinking about this large body of work written by Americans for whom Jewishness was central, and wondering how well it actually has transformed testament into a literature that will last. What, after all, can the ultimate achievement be of a body of prose riddled through with an anxiety that is nonstop complaint, an irony that barely masks supplication, and the kind of satire that deprives all but the narrator of empathy? How deep can it go, how far can it reach, how long endure?

And oh, yes, another thought I've had: how was it that it had never occurred to me, when I was coming of age as a writer, to place my own work within the context of Jewishness-in-America?

———

ONE OF THE WRITERS I read as a young woman who now seems emblematic of a moment in its history when Jewish-American writing hung delicately in some cultural balance, hovering between the passivity of the past and the chutzpah of the future, is Delmore Schwartz. When I was young I read him as a clear instance of literary arrival, today I do not; but today I see his work as if its author knew where his kind of writing was headed, and he balked at going there.

Born in 1913 in Brooklyn into a household where more Yiddish than English was spoken, and the family relation to the world was characterized by a mix of crude and shrewd common to those not at home in the culture they inhabit, Delmore—everyone called him Delmore so I will, too—became an epitome of this arriviste generation of Jewish intellectuals whose writing was both precocious and reverential, at one and the same time an original and a keeper of the culture.

By the time he was in his mid-twenties, Delmore was a presence among the New York literary intelligentsia: a luminous wunderkind whose personality—shaped by an amalgam of immigrant culture, urban street smarts, and a besotted adoration of European literature—was marked by a mesmerizing torrent of words that poured incessantly from him. In Saul Bellow's novel *Humboldt's Gift*, we have

Delmore as we ourselves might have experienced him. The major characters in the book are Charlie Citrine (a barely disguised Bellow) and the poet, Von Humboldt Fleisher (a not-at-all disguised Delmore Schwartz). As an introduction to an evening of conversation taking place sometime in the early 1940s, Citrine gives us a taste of Humboldt's talk:

"Reasoning, formulating, debating, making discoveries, Humboldt's voice rose, choked, rose again . . . he passed from statement to recitative, from recitative he soared into aria . . . Before your eyes the man recited and sang himself in and out of madness." First came politics—a long, wild disquisition on Eisenhower, McCarthy, Roosevelt, Truman (clearly, it's the 1940s); then came pop culture: the tabloid columnists of the day, Walter Winchell, Earl Wilson, Leonard Lyons, Red Smith; after that, on to General Rommel and from Rommel to John Donne and T. S. Eliot; then "the sayings of Einstein and Zsa Zsa Gabor, with references to Polish socialism and [American] football tactics and the secret motives of Arnold Toynbee, and (somehow) the used-car business. Rich boys, poor boys, jewboys, goyboys, chorus girls, prostitution and religion, old money, new money, gentlemen's clubs, Back Bay, Newport, Washington Square, Henry Adams, Henry James, Henry Ford, Saint John of the Cross, Dante, Ezra Pound, Dostoevski, Marilyn Monroe and Joe DiMaggio, Gertrude Stein and Alice, Freud and Ferenczi."

Here we have the classic description of the feverishly

talented, fast-talking New York Jew, yet imprinted with the conviction that to serve the literary culture formed by modernism was his vocation. Within a decade after World War II had ended, he would be unleashing all this pent-up brilliance to a culture-changing fare-thee-well, but in the 1930s and '40s—and this, I think, is the ultimate significance of Delmore Schwartz—could mix the high-minded with the vernacular only in private. To write about Jews was one thing, to *sound* like one quite another.

Delmore's novella *The World Is a Wedding*, grounded in a situation that he understands in his nerve endings, is a transparent illustration of both the toll and the benefit that this constraint conferred. Somehow or other, the protagonists, rather than standing revealed through the story's perfectly formed English sentences, seem trapped in them. And then, in one sense it's as though the author is mocking the characters for letting themselves be thus caught, in another he clearly sympathizes with them. We, the reader, experience a startling potential for tenderness in Jewish-American writing that would be thrown under the bus once it came into its own.

The main character in *Wedding* (said to have been modeled on Paul Goodman but surely a stand-in for Delmore himself as well) is a brilliant misfit named Rudyard Bell. To spend one's life making and thinking about literature and its cultural meaning is, for Rudyard, more than a calling, it is a responsibility. As he sees it, it is the obligation of the artist and the intellectual to reject the allure of mass and middlebrow culture because those cultures foretell the death of literature as we know it. It is, equally, Rudyard tells himself, the task of the critic to preserve for the common reader the culture within oneself that makes poetry flourish. When Rudyard graduates from college, at the height of the Great Depression, he decides his writing is too important for him to try to get a job. He will stay home and write plays.

His aunt had suggested that he become a teacher in the public high school system until he had proven himself as a dramatist, but Rudyard . . . said that to be a playwright was a noble and difficult profession to which one must give one's whole being. Laura Bell had taken care of her younger brother since he was four and she said then that Rudyard was a genius and ought not to be required to earn a living. Rudyard accepted his sister's attitude as natural and inevitable, such was his belief in himself and in his power to charm other human beings. Thus, in a way, this refusal to become a teacher and to earn a living was the beginning of the circle.

The circle is composed of a group of self-styled intellectuals in their late twenties, early thirties, who, trapped by the Depression into occupational stasis, meet every Saturday evening in Laura's apartment to lick their wounds;

otherwise known as discussing art, literature, and philosophy. Among them are an unemployed wannabe philosopher; an unemployed (also wannabe) journalist; two grade school teachers; and the owner of a business agency—all Jewish, all possessed of literary ambition. Laura, a buyer in a department store, is the only one making money. Bitter because she can't find a husband, she drinks in the kitchen while preparing the midnight supper for the group, calling out wildly every now and then, somewhat like a demented Greek chorus, that life is unfair. For all of them, Rudyard's refusal to become a teacher and earn a living represents a noble rejection of the crass world where *all* that people do is make a living. As Rudyard himself puts it, "For us . . . it is not so much what we accept as what we reject that is important." This credo alone persuades them that their Saturday night meetings are a testament to inborn superiority.

Worship of literary talent and philosophical intelligence dominates the members of the circle, along with the ever-rising anxiety that others may have more of it than they do. This anxiety induces the absurd imperiousness with which they all speak, and allows social behavior of the crudest order to pass for normal.

One by one, the psyche of each member of the circle is dissected in the mind of another of the story's characters fully enough for the reader to see that each is preoccupied with separating himself, if only in his own mind, from the others, as each has no means of defining himself except against those he most resembles. Jacob Cohen, for instance, the most generous-spirited of the group, walks the streets of the city during the week, thinking about his friends as though "borne forward by the feeling that through them he might know his own fate, because of their likeness, difference, and variety." So what is Jacob thinking?

Francis French is a stiff-necked homosexual who is destroying himself with his obsessive pursuit of sex; Edmund Kish cannot argue a point without letting his interlocutor know that he considers him a fool; likewise, Ferdinand writes stories whose "essential motive . . . was the disdain and superiority he felt" about the members of his parents' generation. Then there is Marcus Gross, an insensitive oaf who, when Rudyard praises the philosophical genius of his own plays (which he does regularly), tells him that his plays don't get produced because they're not about anything; whereupon Rudyard tells him he is a Philistine, and everyone starts talking at once. Soon enough, one of them complains that in all the evenings he's been coming here he has yet to utter a complete sentence, and Laura shouts from the kitchen, "I have not uttered a complete sentence since 1928." Ah, Laura! When she complains that Rudyard, who lives with her, reads a newspaper at the breakfast table and a book at the dinner table and at neither meal does he speak to her, he replies, "Reading is superior to [conversation], in general, as authors are superior to other human beings."

The novella captures neatly the surreal quality of outsiders living inside a compensatory bubble of their own making, sealed in by the silence of the indifferent outer world. Always a humiliation to people of high intelligence and even higher ambition, among these passionately insulted temperaments such isolation breeds the meanest kind of insularity, and lends itself readily to stasis. Jacob alone recognizes the pathos inherent in their situation: "We have all come to a standstill, . . . as on an escalator, for time is passing, but we remain motionless."

I once found the stasis in *The World Is a Wedding* compelling; today I do not. A situation that years ago had felt not only true but important, now seems to approach caricature. Rudyard himself, whom I had admired extravagantly (with all his silly posturings), reads like a poor man's Lytton Strachey, his own tittering unhappiness at not having had his genius recognized more absurd than touching. Yet, looked at historically, the novella signifies.

When Saul Bellow began to write his glittering, take-no-prisoners prose, what he wanted was neither to serve high culture nor to save the Jews from embarrassment, it was to make the page explode with the taste of his own life: a taste that could never have made itself felt through the King's English, it required a language all its own, one that broke the rules, courted transgression, became performative in the extreme. To this urgency every character in sight is sacrificed (no empathy here), but the writing burns up the page. Delmore, on the other hand, neither he nor his moment anywhere near ready for such savagery, was hobbled by the tenderness he could neither honor nor abandon, forever unable to decide how much of his people he was willing to let the world pass judgment on. While he could not bring himself to love his characters, neither could he bear to throw them to the wolves. It is this hesitation at the heart of his writing that defines the fiction of Delmore Schwartz. I once thought it gave the stories poetic vitality, now I see it as responsible for their inability to realize themselves, saturated as they are in a pained self-consciousness that prohibits the writer from fully inhabiting his material. To my own great surprise, I find the limitation not only moving but instructive.

IN THE LATE 1970s I traveled to Israel, charged with the task of writing a book-length piece of personal journalism about the country as I found it: on the ground, in the ordinariness of its daily life. I never wrote that book. I met some of the most marvelous people I would ever know, looked at some of the most striking landscapes on the face of the planet, felt living history in the faces all about me. Yet, however much I tried, during the months that I lived in Israel, through whichever of the various elements of identity at my disposal (Jewish, female, American), I was unable to connect. As the child of Yiddish-speaking secular Jews, the Hebrew language meant no more to me than any other foreign tongue; as a woman, I balked at finding myself in a country more sexist than my own; as a product of individuating America, I could not get past the appalling tribalism of the culture.

One day during my time in Israel, I met one of the country's great storytellers, A. B. Yehoshua, a writer whose work, at the time, I was barely familiar with. A friend in New York had sent him a letter of introduction on my behalf, and on an afternoon when I was in Haifa, the city where he lived and taught, I called and was invited to come right over. He was sitting at his desk when I arrived: a man in his mid-forties with a bulky body, a powerful face, and a mass of curly black hair. He looked up and said in a voice rising on a note of insinuation, "So why are you still living in the Diaspora? Why aren't you living here where you belong?" I laughed. "You're kidding," I said. He told me that he most certainly was not kidding and went on to sketch a picture of my life in the States as one at risk in a Christian nation that, at any time, might turn on me; right now, at this very minute, I was standing on a narrow strip of beach with the sea at my back and the goyim, for all I knew, starting to advance on me.

The visit lasted an hour, during which I said little while Yehoshua harangued me: exactly as he was to go on, over the next forty years, haranguing the Jews of the world who persist in living outside the state of Israel. To this day, in a voice laced through with contempt, he regularly thunders like a prophet of old that only Israelis are complete Jews. Other Jews are partial Jews—Jews who put on and take off their Jewishness as one would an article of clothing appropriate to the weather of the country in which they reside. It is painful to hear him speak so because he often sounds like a West Bank settler with a gun in his hand and murder in his heart, declaring the land of another his land. It's the bully behind that sound that makes one cringe.

In the years that followed my trip to Israel, I often tried and failed to respond to Yehoshua's fiction because I could not get the sound of that bullying voice out of my head long enough to engage with the work. Then one day, not too long ago, I once again picked up an early collection of the stories written by this fiercest of Zionists, and this time— who knows why—the prejudice fell away and I was in the presence of a writer who, demagogue that he was, clearly felt compelled, when he sat down to write, to honor his own haunting sense of human existence over the political rhetoric that governed his public person. I began to read in mid-afternoon and continued straight through to the last page of the last story; whereupon I found myself sitting with the book in my lap, staring into a room now shrouded in a darkness that, mysteriously, felt lit from within.

The stories in this collection were all tales of emotional disconnect, in marriage and in friendship, and they were soaked in an existential loneliness foreign to the nationalist rhetoric that Yehoshua himself spouted. These stories were both intensely concrete and yet possessed of the kind of immaterial suggestiveness that cannot help but deepen the reading experience. They were the work of a writer who, wanting to dive down into those psychic regions of loss and defeat common to all humanity, knew how to make metaphorical use of a situation as local as that of a sick, sweating man awakening in an empty flat in Tel Aviv on a hot summer morning sometime in the 1970s. *This*, these stories tell us, is how, at this time in this place, the creatures we call women and men, just out of Plato's cave, are moving blind toward some vague understanding of what it is to be human. Any reader whose emotional reflexes were intact was welcome to take in the experience.

The composite Yehoshua character who came to haunt my own imagination is a failing academic who's balding, wears glasses, can't complete his dissertation, hasn't slept with a woman in five years, and is walking at an angle down a Jerusalem street beneath a burning sun whose heat and dazzle double the surrounding silence—a silence that only a region this hot, this remote, could generate; a silence that makes palpable—in rude, noisy Israel—the silence within.

A version of this character is the protagonist of one of Yehoshua's most powerful stories, "Three Days and a Child," and his essence informs the protagonist of another important story, "A Long Hot Day, His Despair, His Wife and His Daughter." In each case, the narrator is a man so ill at ease inside his own skin that when the mundane circumstances of his life threaten to turn hallucinatory, we're right there with him because Yehoshua has put us deeply inside that unease: which, as it turns out, is not the situation but the story itself.

In "Three Days and a Child," the narrator is a high school math teacher who lives alone in Jerusalem, sleeps with a woman he does not love, has been working for years on a hopeless dissertation, and now, in the last days of the summer vacation, receives a letter from a woman he once loved passionately (although she hadn't given him the time of day), asking him to take care of her small son while she and her husband study for university entrance exams. This woman has, for years, been the focus of the narrator's extended fantasies of erotic humiliation, and while he now meekly agrees to do as he's asked, it is with a mixture of negative emotions, all the greater for having been stifled, that he opens the door to receive the child. What follows is an account of the three days with the little boy—"end of summer, hot desert winds blowing over the land"— wherein the narrator's spirits repeatedly rise, fall, flicker, go dead, come back to life, now flaring with bitter nostalgia, now falling back into the inertia that is his daily companion.

The narrator and the child go wandering about Jerusalem "stewing in its silence." At the zoo, he sits on a bench and dozes off. When he awakens, the little boy is not there. He searches for the child with his eyes and spots him walking behind three older children along the top of a slanting wall. He watches with apparent indifference, thinking idly, "One incautious movement and he'll be lying on the ground with a broken neck." Not only did the narrator not care, "On the contrary, I was excited!"

Very quickly, of course, he is rescuing the child, nursing him tenderly through a high fever, and now—allowing normal sympathy to stir in his bosom for the first time— acutely aware of the little boy's forlornness. Paradoxically, his own sense of isolation is triggered—"Now my loneliness was undoubtedly greater than his"—and he is swamped with self-pity.

He thinks with despair of his loveless relationship with the woman with whom he sleeps: "We may chance to meet in a crowded Jerusalem street . . . only last night we lay locked and now, as if by agreement, we ignore each other . . . so great is the pity we sometimes bear each other."

He thinks of all the times he has returned to the classroom where "a few moments after I entered the room the sun, too, would enter through the window. The light would glare in my eyes. It was pure torment."

He then daydreams a phone call to the parents to tell them that he's at the hospital and the boy has died, and we are brought to the heart of the matter. In his fantasy he sees:

The bursting into the hospital, assailing the nurses, the doctors.

The meeting face to face.

Her wonderful, crushed beauty.

They at my feet, I at theirs. Clinging to each other.

. . .

The wonder of their not letting me go now . . . They would cleave to me then, surround me, as though their child were in me, of me.

Would take me for their son.

Because love—of love I have despaired.

Because love—of love I have despaired.

The protagonist of "A Long Hot Day," in his turn, is a forty-two-year-old engineer who, due to a faulty diagnosis of cancer, has been returned against his will to Israel after nine happy months on a project in Africa. Waiting for re-assignment, he is plunged into an abyss of aimlessness that puts him on a continuum with Yehoshua's depressed math teacher.

In Africa, he had "lived in solitude, conceived by him as freedom." Back in Israel he experiences daily a domesticity that spells desolation:

On one of the first mornings home—wife and daughter having gone off to work and school—our engineer awakens to an empty flat, brooding on the night before, when he and his wife had retired to their bedroom together for only the second time in nearly a year: "He put his arms about her. In spite of his abysmal tiredness he intended to be with her, to make love to her . . . But she pushed him away lightly, kissed the top of his head, slipped out of her clothes, put on a nightdress, got into her bed. He tried to insist . . . At last he let go. Anyway, there had been trouble even before his African journey . . . He gave in. She fell asleep at once."

Now, he paces, naked, through the house, "enters each room and closes shutters and windows against the heat . . . enters a sun-drenched kitchen and tumbles straight into the chaos left by his daughter. The butter is melting on the table, the milk going sour in the heat, the door of the refrigerator isn't shut properly, jam is dripping over a dry slice of bread, a piece of nibbled cheese is on top of a load of dirty dishes—it's as though a band of hoodlums had had their breakfast here instead of one thin, straggly child . . . He puts the kettle to boil, moves the entire pile of dirty dishes to the sink and starts chewing at the slice of bread left by her."

Slowly, the engineer drives himself to the edge of mental instability—he broods over his loveless marriage, starts napping in his wreck of a car, hoards the letters that a young soldier writes to his daughter—and all the while there is the "sun-charged morning" into which he must repeatedly awaken: "the sweltering air that is making the road wave and contort . . . the sun exploding silently, breaking up into a thousand sparks . . . splinters of light quiver between his feet, and over his head a canopy of coals."

Hardly a page in these stories is free of heat—the sun and the heat; the glare and the heat; the unexpressed yearning and the heat; the sexual dysfunction and the heat. It is there in every story: pressing into the narrator, driving him to experience, in almost equal parts, the landscape and the people on it (himself, first and foremost) as surreal rather than actual.

Inevitably, I found myself comparing Yehoshua's Israeli heat with the heat of, say, Camus's Algeria or Coetzee's South Africa. Their heat, too, goes hand in hand with an emotional unreality that allows people to do unspeakable things to themselves and to one another beneath a burning sun in the middle of nowhere. Yehoshua's heat, however—unlike that of Camus or Coetzee—is neither sinister nor murderous; rather, it is anxious, depressed, exhausted. It's the exhaustion that makes Yehoshua's stories remarkable, even profound. It runs so deep it feels as old as time itself; as though it has been there since the beginning of instinctual life; as though, knowing as we do in the womb what is coming, we are exhausted in advance of being born. I turned the last page of "A Long Hot Day" and felt what I had never once felt reading a single word of Jewish-American writing: dread.

Yehoshua was right when he said that Jewishness as such can serve metaphorically only in a place where Jews do not belong to a social subset driven to imagine itself in hyphenated terms but, rather, are the ordinary citizens from whose everyday life, at one with the culture at large, comes a wealth of suggestiveness that allows the writer to dive deep and come up with emotional gold. It did not occur to me until I came to re-read Delmore and Yehoshua in proximity to each other, that Jewish-American writing—essentially outsider writing—is deprived of that particular kind of literary richness, and always had been.

And now I was led back to my earlier thoughts on why it was that I had never been drawn to setting any of my own work within the context of Jewishness-in-America. It flashed on me then that when I was growing up it was only the boys who were being prepared to become Americans, so to speak. The girls were being prepared to *marry* the boys who were going to become Americans. It was my brother, my cousin, my classmates who were to leave the neighborhood, face down social humiliation and perhaps worse, lay claim to a place in the larger world; we girls were to be waiting at home to soothe their anxieties, sympathize with their failures, cheer them on.

By the time it was my turn to lay claim to something that resembled a withheld American birthright, it was not as a Jew but as a woman that life began to feel metaphorical. True enough, Jewish-working-class-immigrant had once seemed an identity carved in stone but now, in the

1970s, it clearly was as nothing compared with the unalter-
able stigma of having been born into the wrong sex.

LOOKING BACK on those visionary years what I find most
remarkable is that, almost from the beginning, the women's movement was philosophical in its nature, existential
in its grasp. Yes, equal pay for equal work. Yes, pass the ERA.
Yes, legal abortion and an end to job discrimination. But
at the same time, and surrounding all this down-to-earth
politicking, was an immeasurably larger insight within
which the politicalness of life itself was being understood
as one of the great signifiers. One feminist perspective
after another—from psychologists, historians, political sci-
entists, and literary critics—seemed to be addressing the
whole of the human condition in its analysis of the insecurity and defensiveness at the heart of the social conventions
that subordinated women. Society's unspoken agreement
that women would live a half life in order that men might
have the courage to pursue a whole one was suddenly
understood in the light of anxieties that ran deep. These
anxieties made it very nearly impossible to sustain without
derangement the suspicion that one was, indeed, alone in
the universe. Recognition of the fear of human loneliness
as a motive force for sexism began to prevail among those of
us who cared to think about original causes. And very soon

we discovered that we were hardly the first feminists to have made the same connections.

I HARDLY KNEW who Elizabeth Cady Stanton was—a nineteenth-century suffragist? a friend of Susan B. Anthony's?—when, sometime in that crucial decade, a feminist put into my hands "The Solitude of Self," Stanton's last public address, and I experienced both the shock and the excitement of realizing "We've been here before."

The time was January 1892, the place a packed convention hall in Washington, D.C. Elizabeth Stanton, at the lectern, was about to step down from the presidency of the National American Woman Suffrage Association. This would be her last public speech as the head of the movement. She looked out at the few thousand faces gathered before her. Many of them she had been gazing at for the past forty years, and for most of those years she and they had been as one; but the fight for suffrage had grown steadily more conservative while she had remained an unaltered radical, and by now she had been feeling this separation between herself and her beloved movement for a very long time. It had induced in her a terrible loneliness, unlike any that she had ever known, but the isolation had proved revelatory: she had come to understand emotionally what before she had understood with her reasoning alone.

The bonds of human connection, she had always known, are fragile, subject to time, circumstance, and the mystery of altering sympathies, but she had never before doubted that connection was the norm: to find oneself alone, without steady or permanent attachment, was to lay oneself open to the dreaded charge of abnormality. Now, suddenly, it flashed on her that loneliness was the norm, connection the ideal, the exception not the rule in the human condition. The long, rich devotion to women's rights had given her many extraordinary insights, but none more powerful or suggestive than this one:

"No matter how much women prefer to lean," she began, "to be protected and supported, nor how much men desire to have them do so, they must make the voyage of life alone . . . It matters not whether the solitary voyager is man or woman; nature, having endowed them equally, leaves them to their own skill and judgment in the hour of danger, and, if not equal to the occasion, alike they perish."

In a long life, she said, she had come to realize that nature colluded with culture to the very largest degree in the matter of unwanted solitude. She saw that human beings are locked from birth into a psychology of shame, inexplicable and puzzling, that contributes to our inability to seek the consolation of company in our worst hours of need. We are *embarrassed* by our own vulnerability:

Our most bitter disappointments, our brightest hopes and ambitions are known only to ourselves . . . We ask no sympathy from others in the anxiety and agony of a broken friendship or shattered love. When death sunders our nearest ties, alone we sit in the shadow of our affliction. Alike amid the greatest triumphs and darkest tragedies of life we walk alone.

As she was a political animal to her fingertips, she could not help but associate these thoughts to the necessity for political equality for women: The strongest reason that she, Stanton, knew for giving women every means of enlarging their sphere of action is the ultimate solitariness of every life. And it is from this perspective that she now speaks directly to the consequence of withholding the rights of citizens who are women:

The talk of sheltering woman from the fierce storms of life is the sheerest mockery, for they beat on her from every point of the compass, just as they do on man, and with more fatal results, for he has been trained to protect himself, to resist, and to conquer. Such are the facts in human experience . . . rich and poor, intelligent and ignorant, wise and foolish, virtuous and vicious, man and woman; it is ever the same, each soul must depend wholly on itself . . . In the long, weary march, each one walks alone.

This is a solitude which each and every one of us had always carried with him, more inaccessible than the ice-cold mountains, more profound than the midnight sea; the solitude of self. Our inner being which we call ourself, no eye nor touch of man or angel has ever pierced. Such is individual life. Who, I ask you, can take, dare take on himself the rights, the duties, the responsibilities of another human soul?

Nothing in Jewish-American writing ever gave me back as penetrating a sense of myself, trapped both in nature and in history, as did "The Solitude of Self." I read it as if it was poetry: that's how much like "the thing itself" it felt.

Six

———

Tolstoy once said that if he was asked to write on social or political questions, he would not waste one word on the subject, but if asked to write a book which twenty years from the time it was written would make people laugh and cry and love life more, to this he would bend all his efforts.

A writer whose work has often made me love life more is Natalia Ginzburg. Reading her, as I have repeatedly over many years, I experience the exhilaration that comes with being intellectually reminded that one is a sentient being. First time around, my eyes were opened to something important about who I was at the moment of reading; later, to who or what I was becoming. But then I lived long enough to feel a stranger to myself—no one more surprised than me that I turned out to be who I am—and reading Ginzburg again has provided solace as well as revelation.

———

WHEN I WAS ten years old, the teacher held a composition
of mine up before the class and said, "This little girl is going
to be a writer." I don't think I'd ever heard the word "writer"
before and I certainly didn't know what it meant, but I remember that I felt warm and happy hearing it applied to
myself. Even then I knew that what had so absorbed me
when I was writing my composition—that is, sitting with
a pen in my hand, thinking about how to best arrange the
words on the piece of paper in front of me—had given me
something I'd never had before: a thrill. When the teacher
praised what I had written I felt the thrill again and re-
solved that I would go on "writing." What I didn't know,
couldn't know, was that I would feel compelled to go on
even if what I wrote received no praise, and had no especial
effect on anyone other than myself.

It soon developed that writing became central to my
life. That is, I found that when I sat down to write, the
me who entertained a myriad of anxieties and insecurities
seemed to disappear. There, at the desk, with a piece of
paper in front of me, my fingers now on a keyboard, wholly
absorbed by the effort to order my thoughts, I felt safe, centered, untouchable: at once both excited and at peace, no
longer distracted or unfocused or hungry for the things I
didn't have. All that I needed was there in the room with
me. *I* was there in the room with me. Nothing else in my

life—neither love nor the promise of wealth or fame or even good health—would ever match the feeling of being alive to myself—*real* to myself—that writing gave me.

Of course it was great novels I was going to write— large, dramatic, world-changing novels that would make the reader love life more after my book had been read— and discovered soon enough I had no talent for telling a tale that was concocted out of wholly imagined cloth. When I tried to write such a story, I soon found myself drowning in a muddle of verbiage from which I could make nothing of literary value emerge: the paragraphing was arbitrary, the sentences rang false, the words lay dead on the page. Writing a letter I sounded more natural to myself. It seemed that it was only when the un-surrogated me was narrating that the waves consented to part and I could walk on water: which is how it felt when the writing flowed.

What to do? I was now well into my late twenties and hadn't a clue as to how I was going to write the great American novel when I couldn't make anything fictional come to life. Then I read Natalia Ginzburg's essay "My Vocation," and I saw the way forward.

The essay traces Ginzburg's own apprenticeship as a writer. It tells of how a talented child dreams of writing prose extravaganzas—large and operatic—but hasn't the vaguest idea of how to approach the task of telling a story as she doesn't really know what a story is. She only knows she is going to write magnificent sentences. And so she does:

sentences that describe sinister castles, kidnapped maidens, tyrannical fathers, threatening lovers: "I didn't know anything about them beyond the words and phrases with which I described them." Next she falls in love with phrases she thinks will chase down the ever-elusive story; and after that, characters (really puppets) on which to *hang* the story. Bit by bit it comes clear that the essay itself, the one Ginzburg has written and we are reading, is a miniature *bildungsroman* wherein the author is teaching herself how to grow up and take her place in the world as a human being who is a writer; that is the story.

NATALIA GINZBURG (née Levi) was born in 1916 in Palermo, Sicily, but spent her youth in Turin where her father taught science at the university. While the family was smart, cultured, and liberal, agitation reigned in the Levi household, as the father was a domestic tyrant, the mother a docile dreamer, and all five children given to melancholia. Natalia couldn't wait to get out. In 1938, at the age of twenty-two, she married Leone Ginzburg, a Russian-born intellectual who wrote and taught and, by the time he and Natalia married, had become an anti-fascist activist. In 1941 the couple moved to a poor village in south central Italy as Leone had been sentenced to internal exile, and there they had three children whose birth proved so astonishing an experience to Natalia that she began to write the short pieces that were the genesis of the personal essays for which she would later be celebrated. In 1943, after the fall of Mussolini, the Ginzburgs decided it was safe to move back to Rome: a miscalculation for which they would pay dearly. Within twenty days of their arrival in the city, Leone was arrested and taken off to a military prison where he was put to death.

For Natalia life itself had now accumulated with head-spinning rapidity, and a new kind of need to write came on full force; with it there also arrived a sense of clarity that shocked her writing into authenticity. The trick, she saw, was to pay strict attention to one's actual experience and then find a way to make the writing accommodate it. Out of this precious insight Ginzburg carved the brilliantly minimalist style that was to be ever after hers: a style she shared with nearly every European writer whose apprenticeship was the Second World War.

In 1961 Ginzburg published a novel—yes, she had taught herself to write fiction—called *Voices in the Evening*. The book opens with two women, a mother and a daughter, walking. One narrates, the other talks. The sentences pile up, one on one, casual to the point of disconnect:

My mother said, "I feel a kind of lump in my throat."

. . .

My mother said, "What a fine head of hair [the General] has, at that age!"

She said, "Did you notice how ugly the dog has become?"

. . .

"However did [the new doctor] discover that I have high blood pressure? It has always been low with me, always."

These banalities continue, both in speech and in narration. I remember thinking as I read, "Who are these people? What are they about? Their speech is tiresome, their situation dull, why should I care?" The second time I read the novel I realized these people were actually saying and doing startling things to themselves and one another, but the tone of voice that overlay the narration—hazy, dreamlike, almost anesthetized—was obscuring the action. And then it hit me: all this was taking place just after the Second World War. The war was the drain, the gap, the terrible lassitude at the center of a remarkable novel being written by a writer working out of an acute sense of the poetry at the heart of human catastrophe.

It was the Ginzburg essays, however, coming apace with the novels as they did, that spoke most directly to me; in time, they seemed written for me. There in the essays we had the creation of a narrating persona who, speaking out of the same interiority that informed the fiction, adopted a tone and vantage point sufficiently different that it lent a modernist distinction to the classic art of making metaphor out of nonfiction prose. As I read these essays, even for the first time, I felt myself taking instruction from a master teacher showing me how to become the writer I had it in me to be.

Among my early favorites was the well-known "He and I," an essay that makes literary use of Ginzburg's life with her second husband. On the surface a bold and amusing laundry list of marital differences; at its core the piece is a tour-de-force demonstration of what it *actually* means to live with the circumstantial decisions that push us around most of our lives. Looking hard at one of the most taken-for-granted experiences in life—marriage—historically beloved, ceremonially worshipped, more often than not stumbled into and then ever after endured, we see the narrator trying to untangle the knot of a pair of adversarial personalities (hers and her husband's) glued together in a situation that can seem as though it is being inflicted on the narrator alone: it's him, him, him who is causing all the damage! Only gradually does she come to see how complicit she is in this unholy alliance. At one point she observes that while she has long been holding her husband to account for bullying her with his ever-exploding temper, she has only just now realized that while he yells, she nags—"if I once find out that he has made a mistake I tell him so over and over again until he is exasperated." It dawns on her that the shouting and the nagging together form a dynamic that feeds the ambivalence that insures the irritations that characterize the relationship.

It is the discovery of her own contribution to this disastrous intimacy that holds the narrator's attention, and brings the essay to a point of startling arrival. Extraordinary, when one comes to think about it, the compelling need to bend ourselves out of shape, rationalize trade-offs of an incredible variety, endure a lifetime of intermingled pleasure and pain—all in order to not be alone. The reader's eyes widen as the starkness of the double bind sinks in.

For me, the narrator's discovery in "He and I" of her own part in the complexity being explored was key. I experienced it as the organizing principle behind the piece: the element that gave it dimension and structure, lifted it into the realm of dramatic writing. With this illumination came the one lesson I needed to advance my own apprenticeship.

In fiction, a cast of characters is put to work, some of whom speak for the author, some against. Allow them all their say and the writer achieves a dynamic. In nonfiction the writer has only one's own un-surrogated self to work with. So it is the "other" in oneself that the writer must seek and find in order to achieve the necessary dynamic. Inevitably, the piece builds only when the narrator is involved not in confession but in self-investigation, self-implication actually. To make vital use of one's own part in the situation—that is, one's own frightened or cowardly or self-deceived part—is to provide the essay with narrative tension. This insight was Natalia Ginzburg's great gift to my own working life; central to the education I needed to pursue the writing that I was not only best suited for, but could approach with the same regard for shaping a piece of experience through the personal essay that a fiction writer assumes when intent on exploring the inner life of the characters in a novel or a short story.

Ginzburg's abiding concern, like that of any serious writer, has always been with identifying the conflicts within ourselves that keep us from acting decently toward one another. Like Montaigne, she is fearless about using herself as the specimen *par excellence*, tracing her own development away from the very faulty sense of human solidarity that she has seen at work in herself, even as she first began thinking seriously about the behavior of others. Taken all together, Ginzburg's essays can sometimes seem a veritable pilgrim's progress, as the narrator in these pieces explores the price to be paid for uncommon self-regard.

"The problem of our relationships with other human beings," she writes, "lies at the center of our life: as soon as we become aware of this—that is, as soon as we clearly see it as a problem and no longer as the muddle of unhappiness, we start to look for its origins, and to reconstruct its course throughout our whole life." Thus begins "Human Relationships," an essay that achieves authority precisely because its narrative drive is provided by the narrator's brilliant investigation into her own emotional history.

At the outset she confides that it has taken her most of a lifetime to grasp the seriousness of what she is about to investigate and certainly it will take the entire essay to make some large sense of it. We are primed then to accept that she will be thinking things out as she goes along. And oh yes, she will be speaking in the first-person plural as she suspects that this is the voice that will best persuade her readers to see themselves in her findings.

Starting with the emotional violence of the household in which she grew, Ginzburg remembers how angry she and her siblings became with the parents forever shouting at each other and the house in constant thrall to the father's outrageous mood swings. Self-protection required the cultivation of an emotional distance that, in time, took a heavy toll. In adolescence she began to feel unreal to herself, and soon grew into a "stony-faced" belligerent for whom everyone around her became unreal as well: "Sometimes we stay alone in our room for a whole afternoon, thinking: with a vague feeling of dizziness we wonder whether the others really exist at all, or if it is we who have invented them . . . Isn't it possible that one day when we turn round unexpectedly we shall find nothing, no one, and be left staring into emptiness?"

In time, this all-inclusive sense of spiritual remoteness allows her to indulge the perverse pleasure of inflicting cruelty on others: "The friend whom we have stopped seeing suffers on our account . . . we know this, but we don't feel sorry about it; it even gives us a kind of underhand pleasure, because if someone suffers on our account it means that we—who for so long thought of ourselves as weak and insignificant—have in our hands the power to make some-one suffer." And here we have it: the crime of emotional unreality that will haunt her life and her work.

She grows up, marries and has children, and then, for the first time, experiences naked anxiety: "We never suspected that we could feel so bound to life by . . . such heart-rending tenderness." A crack develops in her armor. When devastation comes—as it does with war and the loss of her young husband, death raining from the sky, children abandoned in the rubble—she, quite unexpectedly, finds herself taking part in a fellowship of suffering: "We learn to ask for help from the first passer-by," then to "give help to the first passer-by." This experience proves transfor-mative. Now, at last, she feels herself real because of "that brief moment when it fell to our lot to live [as though] we had looked at the things of the world . . . for the last time" and "found a point of equilibrium for our wavering life." From this moment on, "we could look at our neighbor with a gaze that would always be just and free, not the timid or contemptuous gaze of someone who whenever he is with his neighbor always asks himself if he is his master or his servant."

Enough years pass that our narrator lives to see that what goes around comes around—and her wisdom as well as her essay is completed: "Now we are so adult that our adolescent children have already started to look at us with eyes of stone . . . we are upset by it and we complain about it . . . even though by now we know how the long chain of human relationships unwinds its long necessary parabola, and though we know all the long road we have to travel down in order to arrive at the point where we have a little compassion."

Ah, those eyes of stone! *Family Sayings* is the memoir Ginzburg wrote at the age of forty-seven when she felt sufficiently in command of her art to do justice to the story she *still* wanted to tell: from whence come those eyes of stone.

"When I was a little girl at home," the memoir begins, "if one of us children upset a glass at table or dropped a knife, my father's voice bellowed: 'Behave yourself!' If we soaked our bread in the gravy, he cried out, 'Don't lick the plates, don't make messes and slops' . . . We lived always with the nightmare of our father's outbursts of fury which exploded unexpectedly and often for the pettiest reason: a pair of shoes that could not be found, a book out of its proper place, a light bulb gone, dinner slightly late . . ."

The volatile father, a madly discontented man with a hair-trigger temper, roars through the memoir issuing arbitrary commands—Sit up straight . . . don't get into conversations with strangers in a train or in the street . . . don't take off your shoes in the sitting room or warm your feet at the stove . . . don't complain of thirst, fatigue, or sore feet while walking in the mountains—for no apparent reason other than an almost demented need to exercise power over his beaten-down wife and children. Throughout the book we never see him as anything other than the sum of his disabilities, a domestic despot responsible for an entire group of people wandering through the years, imprisoned within themselves, intent only on surviving the anxiety felt in the father's presence or, equally, the relief felt in his absence.

The mother, in her turn, having been driven into child-like dippiness, lives inside a pair of blinders, looking neither to the left nor the right only straight ahead into whatever small pleasure is available to her, most often the one she gets from being with her sons: "'Isn't Gino handsome,' my mother would say. 'Isn't Gino nice. My Ginetto! The one thing I really care about is my sons. I only have fun with my sons.'"

Which leaves Natalia, she of the increasingly stone-faced demeanor, standing in a place within herself not quite alienated, but definitely not grounded. Quite casually she lets us know that she is the one child for whom the mother feels affection but almost no intimacy. "In the early days of [my sister] Paola's marriage, my mother cried a lot because she no longer had her at home. There was a great bond between them and they always had a great deal to say to each other . . ." As for herself, she confides, the mother "was not jealous of my friends . . . did not suffer or cry over my marriage . . . [n]or did she mind my leaving home, partly because, as she used to say, I never 'unwound' with her."

Neither it seems did any of her four siblings who remain as opaque to one another—"indifferent and aloof"—in adulthood as they apparently were in childhood. When they meet as grown-ups all they have in common is some grim amusement over the shared past: "We have only to say 'We did not come to Bergamo for a picnic' . . . for us to pick up in a moment our old intimacy and our childhood and youth, linked indissolubly with these words and phrases."

With the novels we know that the story is one of ordinary lives caught inside a devastated culture trying to pick up the pieces. With the memoir, the devastated culture is the family itself rather than the time in which it is living. But in both cases the protagonist is seen wandering in an emotional desert that lends the writing its surreal quality. To drive home the point, the memoir is filled with the kind of disjointed paragraphing that marks the modernist novel:

When [Alberto] came home [from school] for the holidays he told us that when they were at table eating omelettes a bell rang. The headmaster entered the room and said, "I would remind you that one does not cut an omelette with a knife!" Then the bell rang again and the headmaster disappeared. My father no longer went skiing. He said he was too old. My mother had always said: "The mountains! What a hole!" She could not ski, of course, but stayed indoors. But now she was sorry that her husband did not go skiing any more.

It's the tone of voice that does it; the tone, the odd place in which the narrator seems to be standing, and the even odder angle of vision from which she views her own psychological development; the one that tells me Ginzburg is writing to let me know that she, too, is a stranger to herself.

SEVEN

———

Some years ago a well-known critic wrote a piece about a book she had just re-read for the first time since it had been published five years earlier. She was amazed, she said, at how good the book was, and appalled at how mercilessly she had trashed it upon publication. "I must have been in a bad mood," she observed, "certainly an unreceptive one."

Ah, receptivity! Otherwise known as readiness. Responsible for every successful connection ever made between a book and a reader—no less than between people—is that deepest of all human mysteries, emotional readiness: upon which the shape of every life is vitally dependent. How morbidly circumstantial life can seem when we think of the apparent randomness with which we welcome or repel what will turn out to be—or what might have turned out to be—some of the most important relationships of our lives. How often have lifelong friends or lovers shuddered to think, "If I had met you at any other time . . ." It's the same between a reader and a book that becomes an intimate you very nearly did not encounter with an open mind or a welcoming heart because you were not in the right mood; that is, in a state of readiness.

IN THE LATE 1980s I read a British novel set in the aftermath of the First World War and centered on a returned veteran. The book was small and quiet, and so carefully written it approached poetry. A few years later I read another Great War novel, this one revolving around the patients in a hospital reserved for "shell-shocked" soldiers, and as large and raw as the first had been small and exquisite. The two books in question are J. L. Carr's *A Month in the Country* and Pat Barker's *Regeneration* (the first book in her World War I trilogy). The odd thing here is that when I re-read them both recently, I had the uncanny sensation that the large one (*Regeneration*) was commanding me to give the small one (*A Month in the Country*) a kind of attention that I had previously denied it: whole rather than partial. Here's what I mean:

In a brief foreword to *A Month in the Country*, its author said that his idea, when he began the book, was to write "an easy-going story," a "rural idyll" about an event in his life that had taken place half a century earlier. At the end of the foreword, however, he observed that imperceptibly, as he wrote, he saw the tone of voice he'd given the narrator changing and his own original intention somehow "slipping away," until at last he found himself "looking through another window at a darker landscape inhabited by neither the present nor the past." When I read the novel in the 1980s, I ignored these authorial words of warning and for years have remembered only the "rural idyll" part of Carr's declaration of intent.

A Month in the Country begins with the narrator recalling the summer of 1920 when, returned from the war, he finds himself standing in the middle of nowhere: broke, unemployed, abandoned by a faithless wife, and without a glimmer of an idea of how to pick up the pieces. He reads an advertisement announcing that in a village in Yorkshire a corner of what is thought to be a medieval mural has been uncovered beneath the whitewashed walls of the church, and a restorer of such paintings is wanted. As it happens, our narrator (Tom Birkin) is trained at this sort of work. His application for the job is accepted, and he travels north. The story the book tells is of that memorable summer.

Now here again, I remembered the narrator's elation at getting the job but not the crucial circumstance from which he is being rescued: "The marvelous thing was coming into this haven of calm water and, for a season, not having to worry my head with anything but uncovering their wall-painting for them. And, afterwards, perhaps I could make a new start, forget what the War and the rows with Vinny [the absconded wife] had done to me and begin where I'd left off. This is what I need, I thought—a new start and, afterwards, maybe I won't be a casualty anymore." When I re-read the book I saw that I had forgotten the last phrase of the last sentence: "maybe I won't be a casualty anymore"; all I remembered was "make a new start."

Tom takes up residence in the bell tower of the church, lives on bread and cheese, and spends his time patiently working on the fourteenth-century Day of Judgment mural he is slowly lifting from centuries of whitewash burial. In between his all-absorbing labors, he interacts with the various villagers who troop into the church to take a look at him. First comes his employer, the stiff-necked vicar, Rev. J. G. Keach; then there is Moon, a vet like himself, also being paid to recover something lost to time; after that come the Ellerbecks, a family of hearty locals who welcome Tom into their midst, insisting he share family meals and holidays with them; and finally, there is Keach's wife, the beautiful, unhappy Alice with whom Tom will fall into a dream of desire that runs parallel to the restorative sense of life that work on the mural is slowly but steadily exerting on him. The promise of the narrative is that these twin developments will drive a wedge between Tom and his overriding sense of being permanently becalmed.

We know early on that Tom is a survivor of the horrifying battle of Passchendaele, from which he has emerged with a stammer and a twitch, but we also know that he did not come out of the war a nihilist: "when we'd dragged ourselves back from the bloodiness, life had seemed brighter than we'd remembered it." Unlike Moon, who's something of a cynical slacker, Tom cannot help taking the work seriously; and because he does, very early the restoration starts to come alive for him: "By the end of the second day a very fine head [of Christ] was revealed . . . This was no catalogue Christ, insufferably ethereal. This was a wintry hard-liner. Justice, yes there would be justice. But not mercy . . ." There's a lack of religious banality in the painting that thrills and surprises him: the virtuous in it are seen as "smug [and] uninteresting," especially when set beside "the liveliness of their brethren condemned to the torment."

The joy Tom feels over every element of the restoration process is palpable. To begin with, there is the pleasure he takes in the materials themselves: "The second magnate's cloak was a splendid garment—red outside and green lining. A very good red, the best in fact, no expense spared." And then, day by day, as he becomes more and more engrossed by the work, an ability to look deeply into the life he sees in the painting sets in, and very quickly he foresees its potential benefits. "What I'm really getting at," he confides in us, "is that . . . they weren't us in fancy dress, mouths full of thees and thous, quoths, prithees and zounds. They had no more than a few entertaining distractions to take their minds off death and birth, sleep and work, and their prayers to the almighty father and his stricken son when things got too awful. So, in my job it helps if you can . . . see or guess at grubby faces staring up at the only picture they'll see till next time they see it—well, then you put that bit extra into the job, you go at it with emotion as well as diluted hydrochloric."

And voilà: by summer's end the mural stands fully revealed, and Tom feels himself in the presence of a masterpiece: "It was breathtaking . . . A tremendous waterfall of color, the blues of the apex falling, then seething into a turbulence of red; like all truly great works of art, hammering you with its whole before beguiling you with its parts." This is Tom's moment of glory, the only one he allows himself: the privilege of the informed insider standing alone with the painting's greatness "before the *Times* art critic catches on and signals that here's an iconographic wonder for the academic parasites to suck out the magic."

While the mural vibrates with human intercourse, his own progress in that direction stagnates. Here, what is wanted is direct action: something we gradually come to see Tom cannot engage with. Alice Keach, herself going under as the vicar's wife, is as drawn to Tom as he is to her. Repeatedly, he longs to face directly into the impact the attraction is having on both of them; repeatedly, his courage fails him; repeatedly, the tension between them threatens to exhaust itself. One day Alice asks Tom if he believes in

hell on earth—he *knows* she is speaking of her marriage—
and he equivocates badly, hemming and hawing about how
it all depends, hell is different things for different people.
Very quickly she retreats—Oh, I'm sorry, that was a silly
question—and he knows that now he has really dropped
the ball. This clearly was a moment when "I should have put
out a hand and taken her arm and said, 'Here I am. Ask me.
Now. The real question! Tell me. While I'm here. Ask me
before it's too late.'"

A dreamy kind of sorrowing begins to overtake the narrative. The leak in Tom's spirit is acquiring existential poignancy. The summer ends, the work is done, Tom is ready
to leave the village. Alice comes to say goodbye and for the
first time climbs up into the bell tower to stand with him,
looking out at the world now about to divide them. Both
are nearly expiring from the tension of undeclared feeling.
Then Tom, standing behind Alice, turns to point out the
exact place where Moon had been working:

She also turned so that her breasts were pressing against
me. And, although we both looked outwards across the
meadow, she didn't draw away as quite easily she could
have done, [and I knew that I should have] lifted an arm
and taken her shoulder, turned her face and kissed her. It
was that kind of day. It was why she'd come. Then every-
thing would have been different. My life, hers. We would
have had to speak and say aloud what both of us knew

and then, maybe, turned from the window and lain down together on my makeshift bed. Afterwards, we would have gone away, maybe on the next train. My heart was racing. I was breathless. She leaned on me, waiting. And I did nothing and said nothing.

The heartbreak of all the unlived lives that ever were is inscribed in this passage, the melancholy thick enough to cut with a knife. The glory of the book is that as one takes in its terrible finality, its power is made to feel almost original, there since the beginning of recorded time; humanity, from the start, insufficiently provided with the wherewithal to believe in itself.

AT ONE POINT in *Regeneration* the poet Wilfred Owen, a character in the novel, observes that the war poems of Siegfried Sassoon, also a character, are very short. "Well," Sassoon explains, "it doesn't lend itself to epics, does it?" But later on in the novel Sassoon himself observes, "Sometimes when you're alone, in the trenches, I mean, at night you get the sense of something *ancient*. As if the trenches had always been there . . . It's as if all other wars had somehow . . . distilled themselves into this war, and that makes it something you . . . almost can't challenge." Then and there, this war—the Great War, the War to End All Wars—does indeed begin to seem epic.

The time is 1917, the place is Craiglockhart War Hospital, an institution situated some miles from Edinburgh that the British set up specifically to treat soldiers suffering the mental collapse—then called "shell-shock"—brought on by their participation in the war still raging in France. The characters in the novel are the soldiers themselves—some of them (Owen and Sassoon, for instance), as historically real as Craiglockhart itself, most of them (in particular, one Billy Prior) marvelously imagined. Presiding over the whole of things is W.H.R. Rivers, the (actual) anthropologist doctor who emerged from the war one of the first psychoanalysts to understand that the damaged men who were his patients at Craiglockhart were not cowards or malingerers; they were simply living proof of what can happen to people who survive the experience of one half of the world setting out to murder the other half.

At Craiglockhart grown men stammered, screamed, hallucinated by the hour; or went mute for months at a time; or sat staring into something only they could see; or trembled in terror when either a parent or a wife entered the room. Among these deracinated souls is:

Burns, who shakes violently, refuses to eat, and throws up nightly when awakened from a repetitious nightmare.

Willard, who is glued to a wheelchair, insisting, against all medical evidence, that he cannot walk.

Anderson, a doctor who can no longer stand the sight of blood—the thought of returning to medicine makes him shudder—and is discovered one day lying on the floor in a pool of his own urine: *his* nightmares keep the whole floor awake.

And then there is the singular Billy Prior, who arrives mute at the hospital and for the longest time replies to any question put to him by writing I DON'T REMEMBER on a notepad.

The novel turns on the character of William Rivers, the man who is both the most deeply decent of all the characters in the book and at the same time an embodiment of the conventional British need to honor what he sees as his clear-cut duty. Which, in this case, is to rescue these men from the despair in which they are sunk so they can be returned to the trenches. No one knows better than Rivers the bitter irony of the task before him. He has signed on to work at Craiglockhart in order to study mental collapse in people he knows would not have broken down had it not been for the war. So if he "cures" them, only to send them back into the war, what chance is there that they will stay cured, these boy-men who are constantly being told combat will be the making of them. "How misleading," Rivers knows, "it was to say that the war had 'matured' these young men." In his patients "a prematurely aged man and a fossilized schoolboy seemed to exist side by side," a phenomenon that gave them "a curiously ageless quality, but 'maturity' was hardly the word for it."

Most of the reviews surrounding the original publication of *Regeneration* posited the relationship between Rivers and Siegfried Sassoon as central to the novel's narrative development, but it was never my impression that this is the connection that carries the burden of its author's intent. The conversations between Rivers and the famous poet are the most intellectually sophisticated in *Regeneration*, but it is in the relation between Rivers and Billy Prior, and in the characterization of Prior himself, that the real power of the book is to be found.

All the patients at Craiglockhart are officers of the educated middle and upper classes. Among them, Billy is a social anomaly, an officer who is street-smart working-class. Possessed of an intelligence built to calculate the winning odds in any situation he confronts, Billy is cunning, sensual, and if need be criminal: sexually wild, infused with class hatred, devoted to survival at all costs. Nonetheless, the war has brought him to a level of alienation even he never imagined himself capable of. Raised in the slums of the urban north, Billy had always considered England's mean-spirited class system the one true enemy of life. But now, after France and the trenches, he sees all of humanity as an existential horror. The question of how and whether Billy—in all his thrilling misanthropy—will make his way back into the company of the living is the beating heart of the book's matter. Two moments in Billy's life with Sarah, a munitions worker he picks up in a cafe in Edinburgh, indicate the scope of the problem it has set itself:

On their first date they take a walk down at the seaside. Sarah, a wonderfully vital young woman, instantly responds to the holiday-like atmosphere, and we read: "She belonged with the pleasure-seeking crowds. He both envied and despised her, and was quite coldly determined to *get* her. They owed him something, all of them, and she would pay." Later on in the novel, when he falls in love with her and she has become his sole source of comfort, Billy considers telling Sarah what it was *really* like in the trenches and then decides against it: "Somehow if she'd known the worst parts, she couldn't have gone on being a haven for him . . . He needed her ignorance to hide in. Yet, at the same time, he wanted to know and be known as deeply as possible. And the two desires were irreconcilable."

The crucial relationship, of course, is with Rivers. It is during their analytic sessions that the unspeakable cost of the war—the cost to the human dream of wholeness—is driven home to the reader. Here, not only do every one of Billy's emotional contradictions come into play, the sessions themselves demonstrate brilliantly why the most ordinary of analyses might despair of approaching integrity.

Billy is the analysand from hell, the clever patient who runs rings around the doctor, as though, together, they are playing a game of winning or losing. Billy himself cannot, of course, help being determined on "winning." His greatest joys occur when he seems to triumph over

Rivers, whom he comes to love but cannot help seeing as an Establishment figure, as saturated in self-deception as any other.

Like many of the men at Craiglockhart, Billy (once he recovers his voice) is afflicted with a fearful stammer. When he discovers that Rivers also stammers, he is gleeful. Rivers, understandably, claims that his stammer is different from the stammer of the patients. Whereupon Billy observes, "Now that is lucky, isn't it? Lucky for you, I mean. Because if your stammer *was* the same as theirs—you might actually have to sit down and work out what it is you've spent fifty years trying not to say."

As a psychoanalyst, Rivers knows that he must make Billy remember—and live through—the attack after which he lost his voice, but session after session like the one about stammering leaves him exhausted and often crucially discouraged. For the longest time Billy keeps saying, "I've told you, I don't remember." Then, suddenly, he seems to relent. "Yes," he says one day, "it was exactly like any other attack . . . You wait, you try to calm down anybody who's obviously shitting himself or on the verge of throwing up. You hope you won't do either of those things yourself." As he speaks, Rivers looks askance. Suddenly, he knows that Billy is throwing him a bone. When Billy sees the light go on in his eyes, he laughs mockingly and Rivers feels the deadly truth of the moment: "He [Billy] seemed to be saying, 'All right. You can make me dredge up the horrors, you can make me remember the deaths, but you will never make me feel.'"

It's hard for me to describe how deeply Billy Prior entered into me. He threw me back on a sense of working-class solidarity I had not experienced in fifty years: a sense so joyfully antisocial that for a moment it scared me, but only for a moment. The pleasure I had once taken in the pugnacious certainty aroused by class struggle—you have the truth, you know the enemy, you feel the justice of the cause—it flooded me now, in Billy's company, with a nostalgia keener than any other I could recall feeling. And then, for the first time in decades, I remembered myself watching *Gypsy*.

There's a history in American theater of the anti-romantic musical. It has an ugly little thing to say, this musical, and it never loses sight of it; therein lies its strength. *Gypsy*—the story of a celebrated stripper and the most infamous stage mother on record—is one of the great examples of the genre. I know this because the ugly little thing that *Gypsy* has to say spoke directly to me.

I was in my twenties the first time I saw *Gypsy*, and Ethel Merman was playing Rose, the mother. Merman was one of the great belters of all time, with an acting style to match. In her performance there was no nuance, no complexity, no second thoughts. She was like a natural force, crude and overwhelming: fierce, ignorant, a killer. She wanted *hers*, and nothing, nothing, nothing was gonna get in her way. I loved it. I loved it with a hard pressing love that both frightened and exhilarated me. Here I was, this college girl barely out of the immigrant working-class ghetto, with a sense of the world belonging to everyone but me, yet at a moment in social history when I, and all those like me, suspected that we didn't *have* to become our parents: only we'd have to fight to get ours. And there was Rose, up there on that stage doing it for me. The energy this scene induced in me came from so far down inside it seemed as though it could make its own laws. When Merman reached the balcony with "Rose's Turn," my head was bursting with a sense of payback that nothing could make seem unjustified. Rose was a monster? So what. She was my monster.

The next time, years later, that I was in a theater where people in the audience were screaming with joy because some monster up there on the screen was doing it for them, the theater was a movie house and all around me young black men and women were calling out, "Kill him! Kill him!" and laughing "fit to die." For a moment I was startled, but the moment passed quickly enough. I turned in my seat and saw, in the faces all around me, the simple, irreducible clarity I myself had once felt. They had the truth, they knew the enemy, they felt the justice of their cause: no nuance, no complexity, no second thoughts. I understood. And I went on understanding for a remarkably long time.

The very first episode of the second volume of Barker's

trilogy (which, for my money, could have gone into *Regeneration*) has Billy out on a randy night in the city ("He needed sex, and he needed it badly"), looking high and low to get laid. When he can't find a woman, he allows himself to be picked up in the park by a man: an upper-class officer, to be exact. As I read on and slowly grasped what was happening, I could feel on my skin the shock of surprise going through me: this was a turn of events I would never have predicted. But soon enough, I'm right there with them. And what happens? When they get back to the officer's place, he (Billy) fucks him in the ass. ("He'd probably never felt a spurt of purer class antagonism than he felt at that moment.") Later, the officer wonders if he does turnabout and asks, "Or don't you do that?" Billy smiles and says, "I do anything." And I said to myself, "Yes! Yes! Yes!"

Then I said to myself: "Are you crazy?"

IT WAS BILLY PRIOR who sent me back to *A Month in the Country*, looking to meet up again with the Tom Birkin I had not fully grasped upon my first encounter with him.

When I again read the Carr novel, I could hardly puzzle out how it was that I had managed to ignore all in the book that clearly binds Tom not to something as fancy as existential determinism but simply to the war: the war itself: the war that colors every thought, every scene, every encounter in the novel, leading finally to a portrait of human damage so richly intimate it distinguishes *A Month in the Country* from all other prose works of its kind. How was it, I marveled, that:

I remembered that Tom had a stammer and a twitch, but I did not remember its vividness: "There was my face, the left side, [that] worked spasmodically. People like the Revd. J. G. Keach brought it on badly. It began at my left eyebrow and worked down to my mouth. I'd caught it at Passchendaele . . . The medics said it might work off given time."

I remembered him sharing a mug of tea most mornings with Moon, but I did not remember that Moon "through pipe smoke . . . would look speculatively at me and I'd see him thinking, Now who are you? What befell you Over There to give you that God-awful twitch? Are you here to try to crawl back into the skin you had before they pushed you through the mincer?"

I remembered that one very hot day Tom lay back "letting summer soak into me—the smell of summer and summer sounds . . ." I did not remember that he covered his "eyes with a khaki handkerchief" before he dropped off to sleep.

Then I completely forgot that when Alice Keach launches into a bizarre story of a nightmare the first time she meets Tom, he responds, "Yes, yes, I told her, I knew exactly what she was talking about, because it was like that when a really big shell exploded; the air in a dug-out is sucked out then blown in, a quite stupefying sensation."

And, at a later time, when she asks him if he believes in hell, there actually flashes through his head this image of Passchendaele: "Bodies split, heads blown off, groveling fear, shrieking fear, unspeakable fear! The world made mud!"

When I did "remember" all this, I saw that the very particular achievement of this jewel of a book was the indelible portrait of a man returned from the war that had most resembled hell with a spirit that is permanently stunted. Neither crippled nor unbalanced nor twisted up inside: only stunted. He can see, hear, smell, and to some extent feel desire. Only he cannot feel it strongly enough to act. He will never again feel strongly enough to act. He is spiritually stunted.

And suddenly I knew that this was how Billy Prior would have ended up, had he lived (which he didn't), because he, like Tom, would have come out of the war also permanently stunted: "You will never make me feel." The class hatred that fueled his *raison d'être* would have hardened steadily around an inner life grown smaller and smaller; sleeping with women or upper-class men for "revenge" would become routine; family life would not make a dent in him. Thrown back on a self that, increasingly, wasn't there he would have continued to have his unchanging truth, know his lockstep enemy, never doubt the justice of his simple cause. I knew this because I had cheered on Rose in *Gypsy* and cried "Yes! Yes! Yes!" when Billy fucked the upper-class officer, and I knew how long and comparatively undamaged a life it took to admit of nuance, take in complexity, welcome second thoughts.

In service to class struggle (or women's rights, for that matter) I have experienced many times those deliciously hard-edged feelings Billy had whenever he was ripping off authority, and I *know* while in their grip one imagines oneself bold, free, *liberated*. But unnuanced freedom is no freedom at all. It's the nuance that makes us act like civilized human beings, even when we do not feel like civilized human beings. Do away with nuance and it's all animal life; in other words, war.

I was grateful that I'd been allowed a life that had taken me from that single-minded bloodlust to the pain and confusion brought on by the gap in myself between practice and theory, the one that forced on me recognition of all the human exceptions to the ideological rule. I realized then that because my life had been sufficiently free of catastrophe I remained equipped with a renewable spirit that had often been laid low but never done in. In Billy and Tom, however, both ruined by the war, it had sickened to a perilous degree.

"It is the death of the spirit we must fear," J. L. Carr wrote in one of his novels. It was an inner circumstance he would write of often, but never before or again with the emotional exactness he lavished on *A Month in the Country*.

Sometimes I shiver when I think that I might not have

re-read either *A Month in the Country* or *Regeneration*, and then I shiver some more thinking of all the good books I wasn't in the mood to take in the first time I read them, and never went back to. I don't mind if I've read only once a book that has left me prizing a mediocrity—I can live with that—but the other way around: that feels oppressive.

EIGHT

———

Some years ago, after living alone for decades, I found myself yearning for something alive in the house besides myself and, to my own great surprise, decided on adopting a cat. My mother's fear of anything that moved on more than two legs had infected me quite early, and for most of my life I, too, have been either frightened of or repelled by animals—dogs, cats, sheep, cows, frogs, *insects*: you name it, if it came near me I shuddered. But now the yearning carried the day, and out I went in search of the affectionate creature who would purr on my lap, sleep in my bed, and at all times enliven the apartment with its antic presence.

It was late summer, and everywhere in the city there were cages full of rescue cats being attended to by one animal rights person or another. Soon enough, I spotted an exceptionally beautiful pair of twelve-week-old tabbies, each streaked in a different pattern of black and grey, both possessed of exquisite little tiger faces dominated by great green eyes perfectly outlined in pencil-thin black, and I said to the woman guarding the cages, "I'll take one of them." No, she said, they're females from the same litter, they can't be separated, it's either both or neither. Why not, I thought, and said yes, I'd take the pair.

No sooner done than anxiety of a high order set in. Suddenly, there they were: *in the apartment*. Like Gulliver among the Lilliputians, I stared at the cats, and they stared back. What did I do now? I hadn't a clue. What did *they* do now? Obviously, they hadn't a clue either. If I made a move toward either kitten, both shrank; a second move and they scurried. Then one of them hid for three days behind the couch, during which time the other one meowed piteously, all the while keeping steady watch at the exact place where Cat One had disappeared. After that there were days when they both hid themselves so thoroughly I ran around the house like a lunatic, flinging open closets and drawers, pulling furniture away from the walls, calling out desperately. I was sure they would both die of asphyxiation and I'd be brought up on charges of animal abuse.

I tried going about my business as usual—working at my desk, keeping appointments, meeting friends for dinner—but a black cloud hung over me. If I was out, I dreaded coming home. If I was home, I wandered around the apartment feeling homeless. What had I done to myself!

It was as though I had longed for a baby, then had one, only to discover that neither I nor the baby had any talent for the relationship.

The worst of it was my keen sense of disappointment: it consumed me. I walked around mentally wringing my hands. I was *never* going to get what I wanted from the cats! They were never going to cuddle up to me, purr in my arms, sleep in my bed. *Never! Never!* And indeed, for a good few years they did not.

Meanwhile—exactly as though I *were* a new mother—well-meaning friends began inundating me with cat trivia; books and toys and DVDs arrived daily, all offering advice, mostly of the kind the sender thinks humorous, on how to get on with the creatures. Truth to tell, this development startled me, and I experienced it as juvenile and more than a bit tiresome.

Among the detritus, however, was a book by Doris Lessing called *Particularly Cats*. A devotee of Lessing's since college—for my generation of feminists-in-the-making *The Golden Notebook* was scripture—I thought nothing she wrote could fail to be of some interest to me. So I began reading this slim little volume of hers about cats, but the book wasn't giving me what I needed—concrete advice!—and as I was too nervous to concentrate on anything else, I soon flung it away: "Another celebrity writer being cute about cats!" For years afterward, almost all I remembered of the book was that Lessing had had a cat she referred to as "grey cat" and another as "black cat," and that one of them slept behind the bend in her knee, while another had been wrapped in a warm towel when it had fallen ill. In short: nothing. One thing about the book, however, did remain indelibly imprinted on my memory: the tone of its prose. That remarkable voice of Lessing's—cold, clear, level to a fault, richly reflective of her signature lack of sentimentality—there it was in a book on cats!

And speaking of sentimentality, it was the cats who, during this distressful period, taught me how low my own level of the stuff had sunk by revealing the ruthlessness with which my subconscious sought relief. One day while traveling in a poor country where stray cats and dogs abounded, I saw a mother cat and her kittens taking shelter from an afternoon downpour under a palm tree. As I stood there, enchanted in the rain, one of the kittens looked directly at me and in its eyes, I was certain, I saw the plea, "Take me home with you." I remember thinking, If only one or both of my own cats would die—maybe one of them is doing so right now back in New York?—I could start all over with the little beauty in front of me, and this time around I'd get it right. Immediately after this thought came another: So, after all, you are capable of the same cold-blooded calculation with which you have so often charged others.

Then, one day, just like that, it was over. Boredom with my own disappointment set in, and suddenly I was tired to death of thinking about what I was not getting from the cats. From that moment on I looked at them as creatures apart. And then began my long steady practice of watching them become themselves in my presence, through their relation not to me but to each other.

After seven years together, they still lick, bite, chase each other daily with as much interest and purposefulness as if they have just met. Whether as allies or enemies, they are always aware of one another. Should an unusual sound occur or a movement seem to threaten, instantly, even magically, whether they were awake or asleep, they are up on their haunches, sitting side by side, making sure they've got at least one friend in this crisis. On the other hand, once a day like clockwork each assumes a stalking position, facing the other across the living-room rug as though they are miniature tigers and the rug the floor of a jungle. At some mysteriously agreed-upon moment, both *spring* and are quickly locked together—hissing, biting, clawing—as though each one means, once and for all, to vanquish this deadly foe, her sister. A few terrifying seconds of this free-for-all and they fall apart, clearly bored by the game, each walking off, head high, tail swishing, in the opposite direction. Together or apart, six times a day they make me laugh.

Then there is the ongoing amazement of their separate personalities. Cat One eats like a pig and lost her shape early: her belly now nearly touches the ground. She is secretive, sullen, and passive-aggressive, but all I have to do is catch her eye and she flips over on her back, paws tucked in, eyes fixed on me, demanding that I caress her belly; which of course I never fail to do. Cat Two remained sleek and slim (a picky eater), and wildly active, regularly racing through the house. She is also remarkably delicate—when she wants me to caress her, she extends a tentative paw in my direction and looks imploringly into my eyes—and a terrible coward as well: no sooner does someone come into the apartment (especially if that someone is a man) than she's under the bed or up on top of the highest kitchen cabinet. Nevertheless, she rules my affections because when she stretches herself along the wall or the window her body resembles one long exquisite column of grey and black velvet, and invariably the sight of her takes my breath away. I remember thinking, the first I saw her thus elongated, "Now I understand the power of a beautiful woman. One forgives her *everything!*"

Although it remains the lifelong need of these cats to not accommodate me, neither can they bear for me to long forget their existence. They are always with me. Wherever I am, they are. If I am working, one or the other plops herself down on the desk between me and the computer. If I lie down to read, they are both soon sprawled or curled on the bed beside me. If I'm watching television, then again there they are: curled on the couch or sprawled on a nearby chair. Of course, they do not remain stationary during the many hours we are together. Sooner or later, one or the other runs into the kitchen for a quick bite of dry food, or circles the room as though on the prowl, or sniffs insistently at her sister's rear end; whereupon the attention is either accepted or rebuffed and both cats instantly fall to licking and purring or hissing and spitting. I don't think I've ever in my life wondered as much about the mercurial motivation of a living creature's behavior as I have watching the cats. It runs constantly through my mind: Why do we do what we do *when* we do it? Why does Cat One lick Cat Two madly for a few seconds, then sink her teeth into her sister's neck, then raise her head looking wildly suspicious, and flounce away as though *she's* been attacked? Why indeed. It's just like sex, I sometimes think. How many times has a man said to me, "Why now, why not an hour ago?" A question for which I have had as good an answer as the cats would have, should it be asked of them.

I still envy the people I know whose cats drowse in their laps and sleep in their beds, but (to quote the famous alley cat Mehitabel) what the hell.

SOME MONTHS AGO, late on a winter afternoon, for the first time in all these years, I picked up *Particularly Cats* and this time read it through in a single sitting, hardly able to believe, as I read, that I had once held this book in my hands and not been similarly compelled. Another clear instance of my having had to grow into the reader for whom the book was written, and for whom it had, all this time, been waiting.

Particularly Cats is 126 pages long and was published in 1967 when Lessing was close to fifty. The book begins when she is growing up, in the 1920s, on a farm in Rhodesia (now Zimbabwe) and ends with her, some thirty years later, living in a spacious house in a good neighborhood in London—and all the way through there are cats: cats domesticated and wild, cats friendly and dangerous, cats beautiful and ugly, smart and stupid. Cats.

At the start, out on that farm in the middle of the Rhodesian veldt, the natural world has pride of place. Before we are introduced to a human soul, there are birds, snakes, insects, beasts of all sorts that, each in its own way, is a working problem for young Doris and her parents. The most intractable is the one posed by the many cats about the place which are forever getting pregnant and dropping one litter after another. It is Doris's mother who regularly drowns the kittens from each new litter in order to keep the cat population down to a manageable size. But when Doris is fourteen years old, her mother falls into a depression and stops getting rid of the kittens. In no time there are forty cats on the farm. Now, everyone is depressed. One weekend the mother takes a trip and it is decided that the cats must go: *now.* Together, Doris and her father herd all but a single favorite into a spare room and, one by one by one, the father shoots all the cats.

As I'm reading, my mouth is opening wider and wider, until I feel it dropping nearly to my chest. Mainly I am shocked because the mature Lessing relates this grisly tale with extraordinary equanimity—not a blink, not a gulp, not a syllable of distress in a single sentence. What we have instead is that cold, clear, unyielding gaze of hers trained on a bit of domestic Grand Guignol as it might be on the most harmless of accidental occurrences, and then reflected upon with almost laughable imperturbability: "I was angry over the holocaust of cats . . . but I don't remember grieving."

Twenty-five years later we are in the house in London, and we are introduced to the cat she calls "grey cat." As a kitten, this is the most beautiful cat Lessing has ever seen: "grey and cream. But her front and stomach were a smoky-gold . . . with half bars of black at the neck. Her face was penciled with black—fine dark rings around the eyes, fine dark streaks on her cheeks . . . an exotically beautiful beast . . . not at all afraid . . . stalked around . . . the house, inspecting every inch of it, climbed up on to my bed, crept under the fold of a sheet, and was at home." This was Cat with a capital C: "Cat like a soft owl, cat with paws like moths, jeweled cat, miraculous cat! Cat, cat, cat, cat . . ." But just in case you, the reader, might think she's become uncharacteristically besotted, Lessing quickly adds, "[T]here's no glossing it, she's a selfish beast."

Then into the house comes "black cat," who, though the incomparable grey cat dominates the household, must be given her due. Grey cat ("selfish beast") had proven not only an indifferent but a downright hostile mother: she kills the firstborn of her first litter and repeatedly tries to desert the rest. Black cat, on the other hand, comes into her own with motherhood: "When she is nested among her kittens, one slender jet paw stretched over them, protective and tyrannical, eyes half-closed, a purr deep in her throat, she is magnificent, generous—carelessly sure of herself."

These cats do not bond with each other but they, like mine, are always aware of themselves in relation to one another. Unlike mine, which display a variety of attitudes, Lessing's cats—somewhat like the principals in many marriages, she seems to imply—engage almost exclusively through the arousal of hissing, spitting jealousy. The uniformity of this behavior, given the delightful volatility of my own cats, began to seem puzzling as the examples mounted up. Finally, it was this passage that made me sit up: "When black cat gives birth and is lying, luxuriant, among her kittens, grey cat, even though she herself loathes motherhood, sits across the room, envious and grudging, and all her body and her face and her ears bent back, saying: 'I hate her, I hate her.'" Something here felt inauthentic.

Of a sudden, I found myself not trusting Lessing's account of the relationship between the cats. In it she seemed ever and only to see at work the kind of power struggle that is driven solely by the drama of the negative, never that of the playful or the flirtatious or the harmlessly transgressive. With all the Lessing prose I have absorbed, never before reading *Particularly Cats* had I seen so clearly what that deadly serious sensibility of hers serves: the willed certainty of a writer who gives no quarter as she stares down her own disappointment with the isness of what is. Behind that certainty lies the self-protectiveness of the born ideologue. I thought then of all the unforgiving portraits of men in *The Golden Notebook*, as well as in countless short fictions, where all men are cookie-cutter unreliable, their unreliability instrumental to the story being told. Suddenly I was remembering how, reading Lessing for the first time as a young woman, this view of men had made me gleeful ("Yes, yes, yes!"), but the second time around, puzzled ("They can't *all* be this bad!"), and then "Waitaminnit, waitaminnit . . ."

It was the self-protectiveness that had now come into focus for me. It was, I saw, the source of Lessing's strength as a writer—and her limitation as well. If she'd been able to cut the world a little slack, it now occurred to me, step back on occasion into a bit of comic outrage or even warm exasperation, her view of animal relations—those of man and beast alike—might have expanded to include some nuance. Certainly, her sentences would have given more pleasure.

NINE

———

I sat down in a chair I'd been sitting in for years, and in a voice made husky by the prospect of revelation, said to the analyst sitting opposite me, "It is only now, for the first time, that I see, really *see*, how devious I've been about my relationships with men."

The analyst let herself look weary before she replied: "Do you know how many times you have said 'Now for the first time I see'? When are you going to *act* on what you now for the first time see?"

I stared at her, she stared at me. What a fate, I thought that day, for the New York analyst condemned to years of listening to analysands like myself, insight manufacturers one and all, who are forever seeing something or other for the first time and, none of us, able to act on what we see. At that moment some juvenile bit of rebelliousness exploded in me. Fuck it, I cried to myself, let me out of here. Let me out of this chair, out of this room, out of this life. I can't do it, *I simply cannot do it.*

Some time later I was re-reading *Jude the Obscure*, and coming up against Sue Bridehead's miserably inadequate explanation for her own god-awful behavior, recalled this scene in the analyst's office. I thought then, "She can't do it either, she, too, just wants out"—and couldn't decide whether to extend poor Sue my compassion or my contempt. I still can't.

Throughout my late teens and twenties I ached for the characters in Thomas Hardy's novels: men and women doomed to endure long years of suffering that end in the most appalling defeat, only because they've been born into the wrong class in the wrong place at the wrong time. Among these characters none wrung me out as much as Sue Bridehead, a woman whose story retained mythic power throughout many phases of my own experience as I watched her struggle (so I thought) to achieve something that resembled an integrated life against odds that it pleased me—for the longest time!—to identify with. When I reread the book recently, I must say that while I still felt as though a stone was pressing down on my chest as I followed the monumental misfortunes of both Jude and Sue, what interested me most was seeing how brilliantly a great Victorian novelist had tracked the resistance to consciousness that afflicts us all through the movements of a character endowed with so much flesh-and-blood reality that she seems, very nearly, a case study.

The action in *Jude* unfolds late in the nineteenth century between a set of villages in rural England and the fictional university town of Christminster. Jude Fawley, a born reader growing up poor and ignorant in the countryside, longs for a life of learning in far-off Christminster. This longing not only sustains him, it colors his entire waking life. It is the dream upon which his expectations of a realized existence are based; the very fact that Jude has such expectations sets him apart from the people among whom he is growing.

After much early misadventure—including an abandoned but not dissolved marriage—Jude does make his way to the city, only to discover that here, in his imagined heaven on earth, he is an unwanted quantity: a member of the class that is routinely denied admission to the university. And now he undergoes an experience of existential proportion. As a boy dreaming away his years in the countryside, Jude might often have felt hurt or misused but not alienated. Here in Christminster, stripped of the dream of life that had kept him company for so many years, he suddenly sees himself as a creature alone in a hostile universe: "Knowing not a human being here, Jude began to be impressed with the isolation of his own personality . . . the sensation being that of one who walked but could not make himself seen or heard." It flashes on him that the men and women around him, those walking the streets of Christminster even as he is walking them, and looking very much as he looks, seem as disenfranchised as he feels himself to be. At this moment, Jude becomes an empathic human being. From here on in, struggle as he may to absorb the meaning of what he is living through, he will always see himself as one among the many: those equally cast out of Paradise. This resonance becomes the source of Jude's great decency, his decency the instrument of illumination that guides his developing experience.

Enter Sue Bridehead, Jude's cousin, an odd young woman possessed of an unusually freethinking mind who quickly becomes his friend and his mentor, warning him from the start against idealizing Christminster. "It is an ignorant place," she insists, "except as to the townspeople, artisans, drunkards, and paupers . . . *They* see life as it is . . . but few of the people in the colleges do. You prove it in your own person. You are one of the very men Christminster was intended for when the colleges were founded; a man with a passion for learning, but no money, or opportunities, or friends. But you were elbowed off the pavement by the millionaires' sons."

One melodramatic development after another—each a combination of forces beyond their control coupled with their own psychological drawbacks—keeps Jude and Sue from forming a simple, binding connection. For one thing,

Jude has never gotten a divorce from Arabella, his first wife, and is therefore never quite done with her. Then Sue herself adds to their difficulties by remaining so ignorant of the demands of contractual love that in a moment of disorienting despair she marries another man—a schoolmaster twice her age—only to be overcome by a physical revulsion strong enough to make her, against every law and custom of the time, flee his house. Now, she and Jude come together as fellow outcasts. Wanting nothing more than to live quietly together, albeit without benefit of marriage, they are nonetheless dogged by social censure, overwhelmed by poverty and illness, and then, at the last, destroyed by tragedy. Sue's emotional frailty compels her reason to unravel, and she retreats into the most extravagant fit of religious mania in all of English literature. Soon thereafter Jude dies of grief-stricken consumption.

The glory and the heartbreak of the relationship between Sue and Jude—in fact, of the novel itself—is the abiding sense Hardy has of them as soul mates. There are many demonstrations of their temperamental kinship, but one in particular I was repeatedly struck by. Jude's former wife, Arabella, suddenly reappears and announces that they had had a child together, a boy whom she is now sending to live with him and Sue. At first, Jude, feeling ill-used, balks: he's not even sure that the child is his. In a short while, however, he begins to imagine the situation as the boy might imagine it, and that educated decency of his kicks in.

"What a view of life he must have, mine or not mine!" Jude says to the companion of his heart. "The beggarly question of parentage—what is it, after all? What does it matter, when you come to think of it, whether a child is yours by blood or not? All the little ones of our time are collectively the children of us adults of the time and entitled to our general care. That excessive regard of parents for their own children, and their dislike of other people's, is, like class-feeling, patriotism, save-your-own-soul-ism, and other virtues, a mean exclusiveness at bottom." Whereupon "Sue jumped up and kissed Jude with passionate devotion. 'Yes— so it is, dearest! And we'll have him here!'"

These are people who experience the kind of connection of mind and spirit that Jean-Paul Sartre might have called essential rather than contingent. As the author of their being so romantically puts it, they were possessed of a "complete mutual understanding, in which every glance and movement was as effectual as speech for conveying intelligence between them," almost as though they were "two parts of a single whole."

Yet this precious gift of spiritual oneness does not, cannot fortify them against those unresolved conflicts that perpetually undermine the universal struggle for self-command. The most painful element of this novel is its stunning demonstration of how limited is the power of shared sensibility to save us from the primeval ooze within ourselves, ever waiting to flood the plain of insufficient self-knowledge. Jude puts up a courageous struggle, but Sue is destined to cave. One would have imagined that intellectual boldness might have insured some degree of fighting strength in her but, as it turns out, her mental bravery is in thrall to spiritual trepidation of a high order: it's the trepidation that does her in.

By her own lights, Sue is something of a psychological enigma. "My life," she explains to Jude, "has been entirely shaped by what people call a peculiarity in me." Meaning: she is profoundly asexual, a woman with a libido that from earliest childhood has been preparing to go underground. Like a tomboy who remains a tomboy, she has always felt companionate with men but never desirous of them. Having sensed early the danger inherent in erotic connection, she has never been able to free herself of the fear that such connection would mean slavery for her. The marriage ceremony alone—with its demand that she *obey* as well as love and honor—throws her into a state of terror.

This "peculiarity" in Sue, as she herself puts it, has been the bane of her existence. Many men have been drawn to what looks like her ethereal purity—all of them certain that hers is a virginal fear that will evaporate once intimacy is achieved—only to come up against the brick wall of a frozen resistance that will weaken as her love for Jude grows but will never dissolve out. Throughout her troubled life, Sue will be pulled around by the agitation that the prospect of sexual love sets up in her, bringing misery to everyone who gets involved with her as she—herself without a clue as to why the dread never lets up—wrings her hands and stamps her feet and cries, "I can't, I can't!"

There's a haunting moment in the novel when Sue is trying to explain to her bewildered and deeply insulted husband why she cannot sleep with him. But of course she can't explain—what is there to explain? you repel me?—and at last, in an anguish as confusing to her as it is to him, she cries out, "Why should I suffer for what I was born to be, if it doesn't hurt other people?" In answer to which the husband himself cries out, "But it does—it hurts *me*!" She stares, speechless at him. She really does not know what he is talking about.

Only slowly, over the years, reading and re-reading this passage did I come to realize that the failure of emotional imagination in the novel belongs entirely to Sue. It is because she cannot see herself as others see her that she cannot fathom the unhappiness she inflicts on all who love her. It dawned on me then that she cannot see herself because she does not know herself; does not *want* to know herself. It is herself with whom she cannot live; herself from whom she is in constant flight.

Racing down a clear track of memory, I thought, What a long road this novel and I have traveled together—and with so many stops along the way.

When I first encountered Sue's devotion to erotic abstinence, I found it thrilling. Her holding herself apart from sexual love—because the integrity of her very being seems to depend on it—touched a chord of response in me that, in my twenties, felt prescient: as though something elemental was just now coming into focus. It was the double bind of sexual love: its attraction-repulsion. Rarely if ever had I seen it addressed in the novels I'd been reading and never as a key development in a major female character. I felt myself intensely sympathetic to Sue's plight. At the heart of her remarkable behavior lay something extraordinary: the mysterious, exciting possibility of an all-in-allness that might be achieved through *oneself alone*.

Ten years later courageous abstinence had lost its glamor, and Sue was getting on my nerves. Now she just seemed sexually frigid, and I was horrified by her grotesque regression into religiosity. At the time, I was teaching the novel in an adult education course and when a smart-ass student called out, "Ah, f'chrissake! Does she *have* to go crazy? Can't she get a job?" I felt myself in sync with the philistine's exasperation. Why, indeed, was Hardy *never* holding her to account for the lunatic behavior I now found repellent.

A decade later, when I again met up with Sue, my feelings had undergone yet another sea change. I had just had an illegal abortion, and to my dismay was experiencing a sense of foreboding I myself found shocking. Somewhere deep inside, in a place I could not put a name to, I, secular to the bone, was experiencing something like fear of retribution. One day during this time while I was out walking, the words formed themselves in my head, "For this you will be punished." I went upstairs and, as though sleepwalking, took *Jude* off the bookshelf and turned to the sections on Sue's disintegration into religious mania. Now I read them, sort of marveling, and I shuddered, as I read, thinking of the wealth of superstitious dread that must sit lurking just below reasoning mindfulness, in even the most unlikely of people. For the first time, I felt, I understood . . .

What was it that I—yet again—was understanding for the first time?

It was the darkness at the heart of Sue's passivity: that willed blindness in her that I knew so well. Oh yes, there was being born into the wrong class in the wrong place at the wrong time, but what Hardy had made radiate in Sue was the ancient fear of taking in one's own experience. What I was now "understanding for the first time" was how deeply that fear revels in its own unknowingness, how mocking is its resistance.

When I read *Jude* again, most recently, I wondered, as I turned the last page, if the book had finally finished saying what it had to say to me.

TEN

———

The other day I was asked a question of fact that I could not answer about a book I had once known well but hadn't looked at in years. Naturally, I thought if I just riffed through it, I'd soon have the information that now eluded me. As it happened, the copy of this book that had been sitting on my bookshelf, untouched for decades, was a cheap 1970s paperback that began to fall apart in my hands as soon as I had picked it up. I turned back the cover and the first page came instantly away from the spine of the book; then page after page came loose and bits of paper from their crumbling edges began to rain down. Soon I was looking at more than four hundred loose pages lying all about, on my lap, on the desk, on the floor.

Somehow, this devastation-of-the-book went through me like an electric shock. It was as though the physical book had been a living thing, and I could not bear to sweep its tortured remains into the trash. I began picking up random pages, holding one after another up close to my eyes as if committing to new memory its fading print, and then to my nose, as if intent on inhaling some essence-of-book. After that, I alternated between concentrating on individual pages and examining the dried-out glue along the spine, as if it held some scientific secret that would explain what had happened.

Suddenly my attention was caught by the sight of a sentence I must have underlined some forty years ago, and after that a paragraph I'd encircled, and in a margin two exclamation points standing side by side. I looked first at the underlined sentence: it puzzled me. Why'd you underline this, I asked myself, what's so interesting here? Then again, look at this one you've also underlined—how obvious!—what *were* you thinking? My eyes drifted to a sentence on the page opposite where nothing was underlined, and I thought, Now *here's* something really interesting, how come this didn't attract your attention all those years ago?

How come indeed.

I began to read the various pages with reader's marks on them; and then I began to piece them together, like an archaeologist poring over ancient fragments to see which order will yield some design worth having been excavated, and soon enough I saw my younger reading self clear enough, marveling at the most elementary insights this wonderful book had yielded up. Very nearly, it was as though I'd written "So true!" all over the margins.

I put the pages back together in their proper order and sat down to read the book anew, this time underlining and encircling in a pen of another color the sentences and passages that *now* struck me as worth noting. Then I bound the pages together with a thick rubber band and put the book back on the shelf where it had been sitting all this time. I hope I live long enough to read it again, with a pen of yet another color in hand.